NO RELIGION BUT SOCIAL RELIGION

LIBERATING WESLEYAN THEOLOGY

JOERG RIEGER

With Contributions by Paulo Ayres Mattos, Helmut Renders, and José Carlos de Souza

Nashville

First published in 2018 by the General Board of Higher Education and Ministry, Wesley's Foundery Books imprint, under ISBN 978-1-945935-16-9.

ISBN 9781791043346

Published in Portuguese as: *Graça libertadora: como o metodismo pode se envolver no século vinte e um (Liberating Grace: How Methodism Can Engage the Twenty-First Century).* With additional contributions by Helmut Renders, José Carlos de Souza, and Paulo Ayres Mattos. Portuguese only, translated from the English by Elizangela A. Soares. São Bernardo do Campo, SP: Editeo, 2015.

Many thanks to Carlos Guilherme F.S. Magajewski for translating this work from Portuguese into English.

All web addresses were correct and operational at the time of publication.

Printed in the United States of America.

Contents

Abbreviations

Discipline (Year)	*The Book of Discipline of The United Methodist Church* (Nashville: The United Methodist Publishing House, various).
MR	Joerg Rieger and John J. Vincent, eds., *Methodist and Radical: Rejuvenating a Tradition* (Nashville: Kingswood Books, 2003).
RWT	Randy L. Maddox, ed., *Rethinking Wesley's Theology for Contemporary Methodism* (Nashville: Kingswood Books, 1998).
SL	Ted Runyon, ed., *Sanctification and Liberation: Liberation Theologies in Light of the Wesleyan Tradition* (Nashville: Abingdon Press, 1981).
TCP	M. Douglas Meeks, ed., *Trinity, Community, and Power: Mapping Trajectories in Wesleyan Theology* (Nashville: Kingswood Books, 2000).
TPP	M. Douglas Meeks, ed., *The Portion of the Poor: Good News to the Poor in the Wesleyan Tradition* (Nashville: Kingswood Books, 1995).
Works (Jackson), vol:page	*The Works of the Rev. John Wesley*, ed. Thomas. Jackson, 3rd ed. (London: Wesleyan Methodist Book Room, 1872; repr. Peabody, MA: Hendrickson, 1986).
Works, vol:page	*The Bicentennial Edition of the Works of John Wesley*, gen. ed. Albert C. Outler (Nashville: Abingdon, various).
WP	M. Douglas Meeks, ed., *Wesleyan Perspectives on the New Creation* (Maryknoll, NY: Kingswood Books, 2004).
WTT	Ted Runyon, ed., *Wesleyan Theology Today: A Bicentennial Theological Consultation* (Nashville: Kingswood Books, 1985).

Introduction

"The gospel of Christ knows of no religion, but social; no holiness but social holiness." And: "Christianity is essentially a social religion, and to turn it into a solitary one is to destroy it."[1] Most Wesleyans are familiar with one or the other of these statements by John and Charles Wesley; but what might they mean today, when religion is increasingly receiving a bad rap, often for good reasons? "Social religion," to use the Wesleys' term, is on the mind of many of us, for better or for worse. Church and theology would do well to keep up with these concerns.

Note that a conversation about social religion does not follow the outlines of the more familiar distinction of "spiritual vs. religious," since the tension is usually understood to be between personal spirituality and institutional religion. The tension that concerns us here is between social religion and social spirituality (or social holiness) on the one side, and private religion and private spirituality on the other. In the Wesleyan traditions, even spirituality and holiness are social matters.[2] This emphasis puts Wesleyans in good company with both historical and present expressions of Christianity, like the ones represented by liberation theologies, which will be addressed in this book.

---

1 The first statement is from John and Charles Wesley, "List of Poetical Works," *The Works of the Rev. John Wesley*, ed. Thomas Jackson, 3rd ed. (London: Wesleyan Methodist Book Room, 1872; repr. Peabody, MA: Hendrickson, 1986, abbr.: *Works* (Jackson)), 14:321. The second statement is from John Wesley, "Upon Our Lord's Sermon on the Mount: Discourse the Fourth," *The Bicentennial Edition of the Works of John Wesley*, gen. ed. Albert C. Outler (Nashville: Abingdon, 1984, abbr.: *Works*), 1:533.

2 In *Works* (Jackson), 14:321, the Wesleys note that "'Holy solitaries' is a phrase no more consistent with the gospel than holy adulterers."

Yet merely affirming social religion, spirituality, and holiness is not enough. In order to discover the promise of these realities we will have to keep in mind their negative track records. Too often social religion, spirituality, and holiness have given expression to racism, ethnocentrism, sexism, and homophobia, all of which seem to be increasing today rather than declining. As a result, the foundations of social religion, spirituality, and holiness need to be rethought. Faced with these problems, little is gained by those who assume that all Wesley meant by social religion was that people cannot be religious outside of religious communities. We have heard it all before: that you cannot be a person of faith by yourself is a commonplace.

In the Wesleyan traditions, social religion is more interesting and more challenging. Social religion is a matter of being in relationship with God and with others, and it is a public matter, as religion, in John Wesley's words, "cannot subsist at all without society, without living and conversing" with other people.[3] These others—and this is crucial—include not only other Christians but also those whom most Christians would rather avoid, like people who, according to Wesley, "do not obey, perhaps do not believe, the gospel of our Lord Jesus Christ" and others who are hungry and naked.[4] This insight is a major contribution of Wesleyan theology picked up by liberation theologies (many of them Wesleyan, as we shall see), and it turns many dominant understandings of the church upside down.[5] Without such relationships there would be no real religion, and the gospel would make no difference.

Pulling all stops, Wesley concludes that those who do not care about others "shall go away into everlasting fire."[6] That should get people's attention, even today. Without social religion, faith is not only worthless but destructive. The social religion in question—or the lack thereof—is easy to identify. It is always public and visible because, says Wesley, "love cannot be

3 Ibid., 533–34.

4 Ibid., 535, 546.

5 See the chapter by José Carlos de Souza in this volume as well as Joerg Rieger and John J. Vincent, eds., *Methodist and Radical: Rejuvenating a Tradition* (Nashville: Kingswood Books, 2003, abbr.: *MR*).

6 Ibid., 546

hid any more than light." Visible and public social religion is, thus, a marker of Christianity: "whatever religion can be concealed is not Christianity."[7] To be sure, visibility and being public is not about getting the word out about ourselves by creating bigger billboards or social media pages; it is about what difference the church makes in the world.

If Christianity is thus about social religion, what about personal religion? One does not exclude the other, but Wesley keeps insisting that Christianity depends on the social because this is where he perceives a deficit that persists to this day; if personal religion is not expressed in social religion, it is not religion at all.[8] And, while social religion is rooted in personal religion, social engagement is absolutely necessary because it feeds back into personal religion and keeps it alive. Social religion is indispensable, as it contributes "to the renewal of your soul in true righteousness and holiness."[9]

The question is, thus, not merely whether or not one can be a Christian by oneself, as an individual. The Christian community also has to answer the question whether or not it can be Christian in isolation! Just as narcissistic individuals cannot be Christian, narcissistic communities cannot be Christian either. If the Wesley brothers are right that the point of Christianity is "faith working by love,"[10] any form of religious self-centeredness contradicts the nature of Christianity. Churches who do not embody social religion cease to be the church of Jesus Christ.

Churches who do not embody social religion cease to be the church of Jesus Christ.

The good news is that in the past years many churches have made

7 Ibid., 539, 540.

8 "If this root be really in the heart it cannot but put forth branches" (ibid., 541).

9 Ibid., 545. See John Wesley's notion that "works of mercy" are actual "means of grace," and my interpretation of it, in Joerg Rieger, *Grace under Pressure: Negotiating the Heart of the Methodist Traditions* (Nashville: United Methodist General Board of Higher Education and Ministry, 2011), ch. 2.

10 Referencing Galatians 5:6, *Works* (Jackson), 14:321. In this context, they also summarize Mark 12:30-31: "This commandment have we from Christ, that he who loves God, love his brother also."

moves in the right direction and are starting to reclaim social religion, spirituality, and holiness. In 2008 The United Methodist Church, for instance, clarified its mission statement of "making disciples of Jesus Christ" by adding the phrase, "for the transformation of the world."[11] But we are still at the very beginning of recovering this essential aspect of our Wesleyan heritage, as mere social engagement is not enough, and not every social engagement moves us beyond religious narcissm. There are big differences between charity, advocacy, and solidarity. While charity and advocacy are examples of valiant efforts to support others, mutual relationships cannot develop without solidarity.[12] In addition to developing relationships, we will know that progress is being made if we hit nerves and get pushback. These experiences link us back to the Wesleyans and the early Methodists.[13]

In any case, reclaiming social religion is a formidable task to which the theological considerations presented in this book seek to make a contribution. No one can do it alone, so I will be engaging Wesleyan theologians who have worked on topics of liberation from around the globe and across the spectrum of Methodism, as they have helped blaze the trail and kept the traditions of social religion alive.

---

11 At the General Conference 2008. See *The Book of Discipline of The United Methodist Church*, 2008 (Nashville: The United Methodist Publishing House, 2008), 87. Furthermore, the *Book of Discipline* gives this interpretation: "For Wesley, there was no religion but social religion, no holiness but social holiness. In other words, faith always includes a social dimension. One cannot be a solitary Christian. As we grow in faith through our participation in the church community, we are also nourished and equipped for mission and service to the world." *The Book of Discipline of The United Methodist Church*, 2012 (Nashville: The United Methodist Publishing House, 2012), 52.

12 For the distinction between charity, advocacy, and what we are calling "deep solidarity" see Joerg Rieger and Rosemarie Henkel-Rieger, *Unified We Are a Force: How Faith and Labor Can Overcome America's Inequalities* (St. Louis: Chalice Press, 2016), ch. 3.

13 The other chapters by José Carlos de Souza, Helmut Renders, and Paulo Ayres Mattos below address the matter of persecution as well. Renders, in his chapter, notes the importance of the notion of persecution in Wesley's thought when connected with religion as a social expression.

1

The Future of Theology and the Church

What Christianity Might Learn from the Wesleyan Liberation and Holiness Traditions

Grace under Pressure

Christianity is not primarily about religion or morality. It is about grace that makes a difference in the world and in people's lives, grace that is potently at work where we least expect it: in situations of pressure. Within Christianity this insight is deeply embodied in the Wesleyan holiness traditions, reflected in many of the Wesleyan liberation traditions that will be introduced in this book.

One of the gifts of these traditions to Christianity is a profound awareness that God's grace is more authentically experienced and at work in the midst of the pressures of life than on the mountaintops.[1] Moreover, this is where God is most actively at work, as witnessed by many of our Abrahamic traditions, from the exodus to the final judgment. What new light does the perspective of grace that liberates under pressure throw on the Christian faith, and what difference might it make in both church and world?

Perhaps one of the biggest problems of Christianity in our time is that many Christians look for God at the top—whether above the clouds or

---

1 On this topic, see also Rieger, *Grace under Pressure: Negotiating the Heart of the Methodist Traditions.*

located in close proximity to the upper levels of the dominant political, economic, or religious systems. While identifying God at the top is one form of social religion, it is pointing in the wrong direction because it misinterprets significant aspects of the reality of God. Images of God at the top clash with the power of God manifest in Jesus Christ, who repeatedly proclaimed that the first shall be last and the last shall be first, and who lived accordingly. The so-called prosperity gospel that proclaims private prosperity and a God of the wealthy and the powerful is only the tip of the iceberg. Too many mainline churches have become part of this problem as well, as we take for granted—often without realizing it—that God is closest to those who are successful and powerful, resembles them, and behaves like them.

One of the gifts of the Wesleyan holiness and liberation traditions to Christianity is a profound awareness that God's grace is authentically experienced and at work in the midst of life's pressures rather than on mountaintops.

The good news is that more and more people around the globe are beginning to understand that we need to look for God not at the top but in the midst of everyday struggles, including life at the margins of society. Here, social religion reclaims the Wesleyan spirit, as it is reshaped from the bottom up.

While increasing numbers of people are waking up, those who struggle for survival in the face of the most severe odds are leading the way in a new search for God. This is happening not only in the Global South but also in the Global North, as pressures are growing everywhere. Even in the United States, many people endure great pressures and struggle for survival every day. Almost half of all children under eighteen years in the United States live near or below the poverty line; 43 percent live in low-income families, of which 21 percent live below the poverty line.[2] And not even the middle class is as secure as it once was, often only a few paychecks away from homelessness.

2 National Center for Children in Poverty, accessed November 2, 2017, http://www.nccp.org/publications/pub_1170.html.

Unemployment is a constant threat at almost all levels of society. In both the Global South and the Global North, upward mobility is now mostly a dream of the past for the majority of the population. In addition, oppression along the lines of race, ethnicity, gender, and sexuality affects millions of people and keeps destroying the lives of individuals and communities alike.

Looking for grace that liberates under pressure is, therefore, a project that brings more and more of us together around the globe. The good news is that as life is becoming more precarious, and oppressive structures are taking over much of reality—including politics, economics, culture, and even the churches—new resistance movements are forming, even in places where we least expect them.

In this book I will talk about experiences of pressure in various forms and shapes, not only from the perspective of a socially engaged person, but also from the perspective of a theologian in an effort to reclaim our traditions and deepen our theologies. The *Book of Discipline of The United Methodist Church* puts the challenge in the following words: "Realities of intense human suffering, threats to the survival of life, and challenges to human dignity confront us afresh with fundamental theological issues."[3] Our experiences of various pressures, including matters of life and death, lead us back to the drawing board as theologians and churches. This is Methodism at its best, reflected in the holiness and liberation traditions.

John Wesley, the founder of the Methodist movement, understood these matters in his own way. In a journal entry of May 21, 1764, he put it like this: "Religion must not go from the greatest to the least, or the power would appear to be of men."[4] Wesley knew not only that top-down understandings of religion are theologically questionable and may lead to false images of God; he also knew that they distort what people think religion is. The nineteenth-century critics of religion in Europe and elsewhere exposed precisely such top-down images of religion and pointed out that

Looking for grace under pressure brings people around the globe together.

3 *The Book of Discipline of The United Methodist Church*, 2012, 80.

4 John Wesley, *Works* (Jackson), 3:178.

they were merely human projections or justifications of the dominant status quo.

Even today we intuitively understand that top-down religion tends to be a fiction of human imagination, where God's power is modeled according to dominant human power. People believe in certain images of God as long as they are dominant; and when the dominant power that upholds them collapses, they move on to model God's power according to the next dominant power. For example, under the conditions of feudalism, God was envisioned as a king or an emperor; under the conditions of capitalism, God is often envisioned as a business person or a CEO.

Confusing top-down religion with all of religion has been a frequent mistake. The alternative, as Wesley himself put it almost twenty years later, is a religion that moves from the bottom up: "'They shall all know me,' saith the Lord, not from the greatest to the least (this is that wisdom of the world which is foolishness with God) but 'from the least to the greatest,' that the praise may not be of men, but of God."[5] This way of knowing God from the bottom up is tied to an experience of grace that liberates under pressure. Here, miracles are necessary and the order of the day, while top-down religion can easily function without them. Indeed, to see God acting from the bottom up amounts to a miracle that few people expect, while action from the top usually leads to the expected results and no miraculous explanation is needed.

This tension cannot be resolved by establishing a balance or a middle road between top-down and bottom-up, despite the fact that the middle road is a fashionable image in mainline Methodism in the Global North, which is sometimes copied in the Global South despite better sensitivities to the problem. In an interesting article on the notion of the "middle way," Methodist theologian Helmut Renders notes that, according to Wesley, only false prophets preach a middle road: "They advise you to keep still in the plain middle way; and to beware of 'being righteous overmuch,' lest you

5 John Wesley, "The General Spread of the Gospel," *Works*, 2:494. Biblical references to Heb. 8:11 and Rom. 2:29.

should 'destroy yourself.' "[6] The main concern of the false prophets is that the faithful not get too extreme, and, proclaiming this message, these false prophets mislead people.

Theology as a Matter of Life and Death

In the more recent history of theology, similar insights have been expressed by representatives of different schools of liberation theology, from where they fed back into some mainstream conversations. Like John Wesley and the holiness traditions, many liberation theologians understand, first, that God's work has to be identified in the midst of the pressures of life, rather than on the mountaintops; and second, that Christianity moves from the bottom up, rather than from the top down. Here we have two major issues that have the potential to determine the future of theology and the church. How Christians think about these two issues is much more important than most other theological differences and the labels that go with them.

Methodist theologies in the Wesleyan traditions have been part of these conversations from the beginning, and they continue to make valuable contributions. Although liberation theology is often misunderstood as a way of doing theology that is genuinely Roman Catholic, this book engages not only Wesleyan contributions to liberation theology but also some of the Wesleyan origins. While the accomplishments of Roman Catholic theologians in the history of liberation theology remain undisputed, reclaiming other traditions that inform and sustain the liberation theme in theology and the church helps to deepen the conversation. The results are fundamental shifts of perspective that may turn out to be of crucial importance to Christianity as a whole as we engage the pressures of today.

In the process, our understanding of theology and, ultimately, of the church itself is shifting. Theology that engages the pressures of life is no longer a discourse of theologians specializing in the realm of ideas, which is then supposed to be put into practice by others. Theology now

---

6 Helmut Renders, "Beobachtungen zum Gebrauch der Begriffe balance, disorder und middle way in den Werken John Wesleys," *EmK Geschichte* 28:2, 2007, 22. The reference is to one of Wesley's sermons, where he paraphrases Eccl. 7:16.

emerges in the midst of real life, where people struggle with life-and-death issues. Consequently, theology needs to be evaluated in terms of the difference it makes in these settings. Of course, no theology ever develops in a vacuum, even if this is not always recognized. The crucial question is where our theologies are rooted, a question that extends to the church as well.

Theology is always tied to matters of life and death, and it is a matter of life and death in the most literal sense of the words. Theologies have literally killed millions of people and continue to do so, but theologies have also been life-giving and defended life. The same is true for the church. It, too, is tied to matters of life and death. For this reason alone, the church is not merely a community of those who share in the life of the heart and mind; neither is it a community whose primary task is to conduct rituals, although hearts, minds, and rituals have their place.

The church is a community that is shaped by the struggles of life and death; unfortunately, it has frequently landed on the wrong side of those struggles. Not only has the church sanctioned killing in war—often on both sides of the same conflict—the church has also endorsed conquest, colonialism, oppression, and exploitation. Yet the reverse is also true. The church has proven and still proves itself as the church of Jesus Christ when it is a community that shapes up on the right side of the struggles of life and death, refusing to perpetuate the often deadly violence of empire, taking the sides of slaves, women, and working people, and providing sanctuary to those persecuted. There has never been, and there is not now, a middle road.

This shift to seeing theology tied to life-and-death struggles may also help us see John Wesley's theology and the Wesleyan traditions in a new light. For a long time Wesley was not considered a serious theologian because he neither wrote abstract theological treatises nor produced a compendium of systematic theology. Based on our argument so far, we can now gain new appreciation for the fact that Wesley's theology was not developed abstractly but in the mist of the pressures of life, through sermons, journals, letters, and occasional publications that addressed specific issues. His writings on poverty and his reflections on slavery, for instance, provide deep reflections that continue to challenge us even today, as Wesley refuses the time-honored efforts to blame the victims.[7]

Similar observations apply also to the theologies of the apostle Paul, the reformer Martin Luther, and many other prominent figures in the history of the Christian faith. Rather than abstract theological treatises, Paul wrote letters to churches that were struggling to identify God in the midst of the pressures of the Roman Empire. Like Paul, Luther's writings often address particular situations and problems and give specific advice to Christians in troubling times, sometimes changing positions along the way, depending on particular situations. Like Wesley, both Paul and Luther also provide challenges to the powers that be.

It might be argued that these theologians are dealing in their own way with grace that liberates under pressure, seeking to remain in touch with the work of God in the midst of situations of life and death. Examples include Paul's proclamation of the justice of God in contrast to the justice of the Roman Empire, Luther's challenge to an imperial church, and Wesley's emphasis on social holiness. Theologies that approach things this way do not go out of style as easily as the logic of the theological market would assume or as the dominant ecclesial status quo might wish. Because these theologies are shaped by the pressures and struggles experienced in the daily lives of large numbers of people, they continue to speak to us. Similar dynamics can be observed in the development of the various Wesleyan liberation theologies that will be introduced in this book, as they further develop the core concerns of the Wesleyan and Methodist traditions.

Liberation Theologies

What we see at work here, therefore, is a fundamental way of doing theology, which was not invented in the 1970s but is much older, found in many of our historical traditions. When I engage the insights of various Wesleyan liberation theologies in the chapters of this book, my main interest is not in looking backward, however. My main interest is looking forward in order

---

7 See John Wesley "Thoughts on the Present Scarcity of Provisions," 1773, and "Thoughts upon Slavery," 1774, in *Works* (Jackson), 11:53–79.

to see what difference these ways of doing theology might be making as the church engages current pressures, pressures that have increased exponentially since the times of Jesus and even Wesley, now endangering the survival of humanity and the planet as we know it.[8]

What is at stake for both theology and the church can be demonstrated by looking at the early history of the liberation theologies of the 1960s and 1970s. Liberation theology did not develop on the desk of one great individual theologian, even though that is the way the history still is sometimes told. In the United States it is often assumed that liberation theology was invented by certain individuals in Latin America and then copied elsewhere. This is simply not true. There has never been a unilateral liberation theology, not even in Latin America, as liberation theologies wrestle with grace in the context of particular pressures.

We can, therefore, find simultaneous beginnings of the various liberation theologies in different contexts, on different continents, and in different Christian denominations and communities.[9] Even the terms "liberation theology" or "theology of liberation" were used simultaneously and independently. The authors who proposed these terms did not know that others were using them at the same time in other parts of the world or even within the same country. And Methodists were involved from the very beginning, giving expression to the Wesleyan and holiness traditions and revitalizing them.

When James Cone, a Methodist African American theologian in the United States, devised the term "liberation theology" in 1970, for instance, he was not aware that Gustavo Gutiérrez, a Roman Catholic priest in Peru, had just proposed this term in the Latin American context. Likewise, Gutiérrez did not know that Cone was using the same term. And Frederick Herzog, a white Reformed theologian writing at Methodist-related Duke Divinity

---

8 Despite ongoing denials of large-scale shifts in global climate, the scientific evidence is overwhelming. What difference does it make whether 97 percent of all scientists agree (the actual number) or whether that number would be slightly less or more? What individual would not pay attention if he or she were told by merely 75 percent of experts that he or she was suffering from a deadly disease?

9 Note that there are also Islamic, Jewish, and Buddhist liberation theologies.

School in the southern United States, was not aware that either Cone or Gutiérrez were using the term "liberation theology" when he published the first publication that bore the title "Theology of Liberation" in the United States, a few months before the release of Cone's book.[10]

From the Asian perspective, Korean Minjung theologians have made similar observations, pointing out that so-called Minjung theology is neither a copy of Latin American liberation theology nor an imitation of European political theology but a genuine expression of what we would call the grace that liberates in the lives of common people in Asia.[11] Even British theologians developed their own strands of liberation theology, growing out of the struggles of the people of Britain rather than out of an effort to copy other people's theologies. In 1995 Methodist theologian John Vincent noted that "British liberation theology has been happening in the cracks and crevices of the land more or less for a decade." These liberation theologians come from all walks of life, as Vincent points out, many of them (unsurprisingly) not "people with much time for reading and research, much less reflection and writing."[12]

Forms of these liberation theologies continue to be practiced at the grassroots level around the world today, and the practitioners include many who have worked among ordinary people all their lives, like the Methodist

---

10 See James Cone, *A Black Theology of Liberation*, 2nd ed. (Maryknoll, NY: Orbis Books, 1986); Gustavo Gutiérrez, *A Theology of Liberation: History, Politics, and Salvation*, revised 15th anniversary ed., trans. Sister Caridad Inda and John Eagleson (Maryknoll, NY: Orbis, 1988); Frederick Herzog, "Theology of Liberation," *Continuum* 7, no. 4 (Winter 1970): 515–24. Herzog, a member of the United Church of Christ, taught at Duke Divinity School from 1960 until his death in 1995. His affinity to Methodism can also be seen in his participation in the Oxford Institute in Methodist Theological Studies in the 1980s, on topics of liberation theology.

11 See David Kwang-sun Suh, "A Biographical Sketch of an Asian Theological Consultation," in *Minjung Theology: People as the Subjects of History*, ed. Kim Yong Bock (Singapore: The Commission on Theological Concerns, The Christian Conference of Asia, 1981), 17–40.

12 John Vincent, "Liberation Theology in Britain, 1970-1995, in *Liberation Theology UK*, ed. Chris Rowland and John Vincent, British Liberation Theology 1 (Sheffield: Urban Theology Unit, 1995), 29.

theologian Gil Dawes, who pastored churches in rural areas of Iowa in the United States. Dawes was able to involve established United Methodist churches in the practice of liberation theology by reading the Bible, considering the deep and countless biblical commitments to justice and to the oppressed that are often missing among those who profess to take the Bible literally.[13] As Dawes tells the story, churches who began reading the Bible again changed within a year or two. Conversion, it seems, is possible not just for individuals but also for whole communities.[14]

This history has profound implications for the relation of theology to church and world, because theology no longer shapes up as an elitist or idealist discipline, devised by individuals in highly specialized conversations. Theology, in this context, relates to communities of faith as they seek to identify God in the midst of particular pressures they are experiencing. Unfortunately, this rootedness in real-life pressures is still too often missing in mainline theologies. The same is true for mainline churches, which often exist in separate bubbles. The good news is that there is an alternative when both theology and church join the work of God in the world.

Theologies rooted in concrete experience are different from theologies developed in the artificial calm of studies and sanctuaries.

If God is sought in the tensions of life, rather than on the religious mountaintops or in the artificial calm of studies and sanctuaries, theology and the church shape up differently. When children are starving and clean water is not available, for instance, professions of God's power need to address the difference that God is making in this situation, no matter

13 See the report in Gil Dawes, "Working People and the Church: Profile of a Liberated Church in Reactionary Territory," in *Churches in Struggle: Liberation Theologies and Social Change in North America*, ed. William K. Tabb (New York: Monthly Review Press, 1986).

14 Personal conversation with Gil Dawes, August 2009. The unfortunate ending of this story is that in several cases Dawes was moved elsewhere after about a decade, and pastors were brought in who returned to business as usual.

what theologians and philosophers have to say about the idea of divine omnipotence.

As a result, theology cannot pretend easy command of universal categories such as omnipotence, nor can it be done abstractly and at a safe distance from actual suffering. Nevertheless, what may still sound somewhat shocking to the guild of professional theologians and their students has a long tradition, of which Paul, Luther, Wesley, and many others were parts. Jesus himself models this way of doing theology, seeking to understand God in the midst of the tensions of life; this is not hard to see when the Gospels are read as stories rather than as pericopes, and this is the context in which his disciples came to know him. The earliest followers of Jesus, both men and women, rarely had the luxury of operating at a safe distance.

Wesleyan Liberation of Theology

Similar to the example of Jesus and to the experiences of various liberation theologies, Wesleyan theology can be understood as an effort to identify the work of God in the midst of the tensions of life. It is widely acknowledged that John Wesley himself was not only aware of the grave pressures of life in his time but that he was also involved in efforts to alleviate them. He did not only consider the plight of the workers, the poor, the prisoners, the sick, and the slaves; he structured his societies in such a way that the plight of these groups was alleviated—not merely through service to them, but by bringing them into the communities. This set him apart from professional theologians, both past and present, who may well be aware of some of these pressures but who consider them of little relevance to the discipline or even as a disturbance to their work. And this set Wesley apart from a pervasive narcissism that shapes many of our churches today.

Wesleyan theology seeks to identify the work of God in the midst of life's tensions.

Wesley not only acknowledges and addresses the tensions of life and death; he also does theology in light of these tensions, seeking to understand the work of God in this context. Wesley's theology of grace—a theme that has been strongly emphasized in prominent studies of Wesleyan theology[15]—must thus be understood as a theology of grace under pressure. In other words, grace is not a generic entity—grace is not "one size fits all"—but takes shape in particular situations of need and pressure, resulting in liberation.

While Albert Outler, the father of much of contemporary Wesleyan theology, was right to call Wesley a "folk theologian,"[16] he and subsequent Wesleyan theologians considered only half of the story. Outler's concern was with a Wesley who was able to communicate difficult theological issues to simple people. But what do we know about the theological insights that Wesley might have gathered from these people? We have yet to see a serious study of this subject by a historical theologian.[17] This question does pose some challenges, to be sure, because if Wesley is understood as someone who learns from others, he can no longer be portrayed as the church leader from whose individual genius Methodism was born. And, equally challenging, a theology and church that learn from others will no longer be able to pretend that they have all the answers.

This deeper understanding of Wesleyan theology can help us to see liberation theologies in a different light. The most pernicious misunderstanding that still lingers is that liberation theologies are primarily concerned with matters of social ethics.[18] The truth is, however, that liberation

---

15 See, for instance, Thomas Langford, *Methodist Theology* (Peterborough, England: Epworth Press, 1998), and Randy Maddox, *Responsible Grace: John Wesley's Practical Theology* (Nashville: Kingswood Books, 1994).

16 See Albert Outler, "John Wesley: Folk Theologian," *Theology Today* 34 (July 1977): 150–60.

17 One brief answer is given by Justo González, "Can Wesley be Read in Spanish?" in Randy L. Maddox, ed., *Rethinking Wesley's Theology for Contemporary Methodism* (Nashville: Kingswood Books, 1998, abbr. *RWT*), 161–68, when he seeks to show the impact that Spanish thinkers like Miguel de Molinos (a Spanish mystic) and Gregorio Lopez (a mysterious author, born in Madrid in 1542, and died in Mexico in 1596) made on Wesley, who was able to read Spanish. Of course, these authors are not necessarily the representatives of the people either.

18 Kenneth Cracknell and Susan J. White, *An Introduction to World Methodism* (Cambridge: Cambridge University Press, 2005), ch. 9. This discusses the Methodist efforts related to liberation theology under this heading.

theologies were, from the beginning, devised to deal with the core issues of Christian faith, including our understanding of God, Jesus Christ, the Holy Spirit, humanity, the church, and the nature of sin and salvation. The consequences of this work are substantial, as dominant understandings of these doctrines are often used to shore up the status quo. Today, for instance, the economics and politics of neoliberal capitalism are shored up by distorted theological understandings, as in, for instance, the "invisible hand of the market."[19] Of course, ethical commitments are not insignificant, and they flow from these discussions, but ethics is not necessarily where the conversation begins.

Liberation theologies are concerned with the core issues of Christian faith; ethics flows out of this concern.

Doing theology in the midst of the tensions and pressures of life mirrors the theological method of many of the biblical authors. This is one of the reasons why the Bible is such a remarkable book—how many other examples of ancient world literature emerged from the struggles of the people rather than the preoccupations of the elites? James Cone draws the conclusion: "When theologians and preachers experience contradictions in life that shake the foundation of the accepted faith of the community, they are forced by faith itself to return to its source so as to interpret faith in a new light and thereby be empowered to struggle against the forces of evil that seek to destroy its credibility."[20] I will develop this insight in the following chapters, going through liberation theologies' interpretations of the doctrines of sin and salvation, as well as interpretations of God, church, and the Bible.

In sum, as liberation theologies throw new light on how we understand Wesleyan theology, Wesleyan theology can help us understand liberation theology and develop it further, helping us to engage our own times more appropriately. To be sure, the point of my argument is not

19 See Joerg Rieger, *No Rising Tide: Theology, Economics, and the Future* (Minneapolis: Fortress Press, 2009).

20 James H. Cone, *For My People: Black Theology and the Black Church* (Maryknoll, NY: Orbis Books, 1984), 41.

to glorify any particular kind of theology. Wesleyan liberation theologies break new ground because they do theology in the midst of life-and-death struggles, presenting a grace that liberates in the midst of oppression and suffering and developing and reinforcing life-giving alternatives, but there is always more work to be done. The work of theology is never finished.

Even though the theologies introduced in this book are rooted in particular life-and-death struggles, they are relevant for Christianity as a whole and even for the world; and this relevance helps us envision a more relevant future for theology and the church. This is the kind of future that we have to work toward, not only because the future of theology and church are in danger, but because the future of the world is in danger. Unless we face this reality, theology and the church will have little to contribute to the future of anything. Ask yourself the question: What would the world lose if theology and the church as they currently exist disappeared?

Would we lose much if theology and the church disappeared?

In this exploration we need to keep in mind various issues. While the theologies to be discussed here have their beginnings in the 1960s and 1970s, the concerns of liberation are much older; they are at the heart of the Judeo-Christian traditions and have been at work throughout the history of the church, though often suppressed. Today, liberation theologies and their concerns continue to be devised and written by new generations in ways that push beyond and challenge the mothers and fathers of these approaches; and liberation theologies are unlikely to disappear until the various tensions and pressures of life to which they refer have disappeared.

Moreover, none of the Wesleyan theologians who will be discussed should be considered as individuals who came up with great theological ideas all by themselves, in the privacy of their studies or in the isolation of some library. Liberation theologies are not about individual heroes who single-handedly unleashed the powers of liberation but are indebted to communities under pressure and need to be understood in relation to these communities.

Taking Theologians from the Pedestal

Theology and the identity of the theologian will have to be conceived in new terms. For Wesleyans and Methodists this means not only that we have to rethink our own work but that we will also have to take John Wesley from his pedestal as an individual hero and genius, although we continue to be inspired by him and learn from him. Utlimately, the theological pedestal needs to remain empty, as no individual theologian or church leader ever belongs there.

An example from my own work may exemplify what I mean. When some theologians and pastors began to read the Bible together with low-wage workers in the context of their struggles, new insights emerged. One of the most pernicious ideas we encountered time and again was the common assumption that God is located at the top, with the employers, implying that workers must be submissive and accept low pay and substandard working conditions. Studying the life of Jesus in the Gospels as well as other traditions of the church helped us challenge these ideas. If God is located with Jesus, and therefore with working people who are experiencing great pressure, we can rethink how God's power and grace is at work in the world: not from the top down but from the bottom up. This insight had implications for our relationships; it allowed workers to take themselves seriously, to relate to other workers, and to become aware of the work of God in new ways. Perhaps the most surprising insight of all was that this kind of theological approach was tied to a deepening faith.

A final comment emerges from these engagements: liberation theologies differ from liberal theologies in various ways. The latter, for example, often play down miracles and other turns of events that surpass the common-sense logic of the theologian. Liberation theologies, by contrast, expect God's power to be able to accomplish what common sense refuses to consider, namely to make a difference where few people think it possible. According to Paul, God chose those who are foolish and weak to put to shame the wise and the strong (1 Cor. 1:26-29), and Jesus preaches blessings to the poor and woe to the rich (Luke 6:20, 24).

Of course, liberation theologies differ from conservative theologies as well, as they are grounded in what turns out to be a faith that expects greater miracles that defy not only common sense but also the theologians' status quo. What is the greater miracle: that Jesus can walk on water or that the kingdom of God is able to bring good news to the poor (Matt. 11:5), so that they will no longer be poor, and liberate the oppressed (Luke 4:18-19)? Wesleyan holiness theologies, despite the fact that they have often been reduced to concerns of individual holiness, share this broader horizon.

2

Naming and Challenging Sin in the Global Empire

Sin is perhaps the most important concern shared by the various theologies that deal with social religion and grace that liberates under pressure; Wesleyan theologies and holiness theologies are no exception. Of the many points of difference between liberation and liberal theologies, this is perhaps the most important one, as liberal theologies have often tried to play down the more severe aspects of sin. When dealing with matters of life and death, however, we can no longer glance over sin, which appears to be the root cause for the widespread suffering and death that affect us today.

The Gravity of Sin

Concern about sin is an old topic, and liberation theologies have some surprising allies. Sin plays a crucial role in the work of the medieval theologian Anselm of Canterbury, for instance, who reminded the readers of his book *Cur Deus Homo* of the gravity of sin.[1] Sin is such a powerful reality, according to Anselm, that not even God can simply forgive and forget. This parallel between the scholastic theology of the Middle Ages and many liberation theologies is often overlooked. Liberation theologies tend to give a more profound account of the weight of sin than any other contemporary

---

1 "Nondum considerasti quanti ponderis sit peccata." Anselm of Canterbury, *Cur Deus Homo*, trans. Janet Fairweather, in *Anselm of Canterbury: The Major Works*, ed. Brian Davies and G. R. Evans (Oxford: Oxford University Press, 1998), 305. See also my interpretation in Rieger, *Christ and Empire: From Paul to Postcolonial Times* (Minneapolis: Fortress Press, 2007), ch. 3.

theologies, both liberal and conservative. Still, as we shall see, today we need to take sin even more seriously than Anselm did.

Of course, the focus for discussing sin is on overcoming it rather than merely describing and analyzing it. However, without a thorough understanding of sin, we will not be able to fight it and to overcome it, and the topic of salvation (discussed in the next chapter) will be underdeveloped and irrelevant. Any naïve optimism that ignores the gravity of sin not only leads to shallow understandings of liberating grace; it also amounts to a betrayal of those who suffer most from the pressures of the current age: the exploited, the excluded, the abused, and the oppressed.

Liberation theologies give more profound accounts of the weight of sin.

It is the topic of sin that most clearly distinguishes liberation theologies from other theologies. Many liberal theologies, for instance, hold on to optimistic attitudes about sin that consider it as limited and malleable. Sin, for many liberals, is easily addressed and overcome by human effort and has little impact on human freedom. Here, humans seem to have a choice in whether or not they want to overcome sin, as they can do whatever they put their minds to. Moreover, liberal theologies tend not to put too much effort into analyzing sin. While they would agree that "nobody is perfect," they often do not feel the need to ask a lot of questions about the underlying causes and structures of sin. The liberal Methodist theologian Schubert Ogden, for instance, once defined *ideology* as the rationalization of positions already taken.[2] Here, sin does not go very deep, meaning that those who justify their own positions are usually aware of what they are doing and can thus decide to stop sinning at any time. Politicians, for example, often justify their positions knowingly and could decide to stop doing so.

By contrast, liberation theologians might define *ideology* as the rationalization of positions of which we are not aware. Here, sin is a much more insidious reality of which we are, for the most part, not even aware but that shapes both

2 Schubert Ogden, *Faith and Freedom: Toward a Theology of Liberation* (Nashville: Abingdon Press, 1989), 31.

our lives and our thoughts to the core.[3] Racism, for instance, functions at both levels: it can be a conscious rationalization of white privilege, the kind that led to slavery in the southern states of the U. S., or it can be an unconscious rationalization of privilege that is more common today, where white people are often unaware of their privilege and the structures that keep it in place.

Unlike liberal theologies, conservative theologies tend to put more emphasis on the gravity of sin, often agreeing with classical theologians like Augustine on notions of original sin. But even though many conservative theologians make efforts to take sin seriously, they tend to define it in abstract terms, and thus seek to remedy it in equally abstract terms. In many evangelical circles, for instance, sin is defined as a total separation of humanity and God, without giving much thought to how this separation manifests in people's lives. All it would take to overcome this kind of sin is to believe in some divine action on the cross that supposedly overcomes this separation, expressed perhaps by saying a short prayer or by signing a card with name and date. Here, sin remains for the most part abstract.

When sin is addressed in more detail by conservative theologies, it is often equated with generally accepted morals, like the prohibition of dancing, going to the movies, smoking, or drinking. Many Wesleyans, myself included, were raised this way so that sin appeared to be some form of immorality that stayed on the surface. Despite a sense of original sin, that is, an understanding of sin that goes deeper and transcends the morality of individual believers, conservative theologies rarely think about sin as a structural reality or as an unconscious distortion that can subvert even our best intentions and our moral actions.

Classical Definitions of Sin

The classical definition of sin as pride may serve as an example of the difficulty of understanding sin. Is pride a matter of individual attitudes in relation to other people and to God, which we are free to either embrace or reject, as many liberal Christians seem to assume when they affirm the goodness

---

3 Joerg Rieger, *Remember the Poor: The Challenge to Theology in the Twenty-First Century* (Harrisburg, PA: Trinity Press International, 1998), 58.

of our human nature? Or is pride a fundamental flaw of human nature that completely separates us from God but that can nevertheless be overcome by an individual through repentance and a prayer for forgiveness, as conservative Christians all over the world assume when they pray the so-called "sinner's prayer"?

There is another way to address this problem. Theologies that deal with liberating grace under pressure reflect on the actual forms that pride takes in particular situations of pressure, and then seek to address the structures that undergird it. These theologies would first address what structures hold pride in place beyond individual actions and then search for God's grace at work at the level of not only the individual but also the community. In other words, there is no easy escape from sin, neither by affirming the goodness of our human nature nor by praying a prayer of forgiveness. When this is understood, we can begin to address sin and think about ways to overcome it.

Sin has implications for not only individuals but also social relationships and the world as a whole.

John Wesley upheld a strong doctrine of sin, asserting a view of the "total depravity" of the human being that is often attributed to Augustine. This was one of the few points where he found himself in agreement with the Calvinists of his time and where he would be in agreement with many conservative Christians today.[4] However, Wesley also understood that the fallen state of humanity has implications for not only individuals but also social relationships and the world as a whole. Where conservatives, both past and present, for instance, tend to blame the sinfulness of the poor for the problems they face Wesley pointed out the role of wealthy landowners in pushing the poor off their lands, thus broadening the understanding of sin to include not only the bottom but also the top and particular social

4 See John Wesley, "Minutes of Some Late Conversations Between the Rev. Mr. Wesley's [sic] and Others," in *Works* (Jackson), 8:285: "Q. 23. Wherein may we come to the very edge of Calvinism? A. (1.) In ascribing all good to the free grace of God. (2.) In denying all natural free-will and all power antecedent to grace. And, (3.) In excluding all merit from man; even for what he has or does by the grace of God."

conditions.[5] Since nothing and nobody is excluded from sinfulness, nothing and nobody is excluded from the need for salvation. Wesley's hope was for an all-encompassing salvation that would make a real difference in the world and that would ultimately amount to a new creation by the grace of God. The grace at work under pressure is able to transform not only individuals but also the world and its particular structures.

When it comes to discussions of sin, it is often overlooked that liberation theologies tend to side with Wesley on matters concerning human depravity in principle. The first step in many liberation theologies is a critique of sin rather than an affirmation of the world as it is. This approach is the exact opposite of liberal theology, where religious experience grants us access to God and affirms our place in the world. Unlike classical liberal theologies following Schleiermacher, many feminist theologies, for instance, start out with an experience of sin rather than with a religious experience that grants them immediate access to God. This experience of sin is manifest in a pervasive sense that things are not the way they are supposed to be.[6]

In what follows I will give an overview of the theological understanding of sin as developed by several Wesleyan liberation theologies. Since these theologies arise in the midst of particular pressures in the lives of particular communities, we should understand them as the fruits of wide-ranging movements that push beyond individual lives to broader communities of the Christian faith and to the world. These are genuine forms of social religion and need to be treated as such.

Note also that while the term liberation theology describes particular understandings of sin and particular encounters with liberating grace, it is not a label that should be used in the same manner that corporations might use brand names. In other words, the notion of liberation theology is not anyone's private property, so it can be used in different settings in different ways. In some cases, it may not even be necessary to use the term at all if it creates defensive attitudes or misunderstandings, as often happens in the

5 See Wesley, "Thoughts on the Present Scarcity of Provisions" in *Works* (Jackson), 11:56–57.

6 See Joerg Rieger, *God and the Excluded: Vision and Blindspots in Contemporary Theology* (Minneapolis: Fortress Press, 2001), ch. 4.

United States. In my own work, for example, I rarely put it in the titles of my books, but I never deny it when people call me a liberation theologian.

Sin, Gender, and Sexuality

Methodist Rebecca Chopp, a feminist theologian from the U.S., laments the lack of a deeper understanding of sin in mainline theology, especially where it is still defined in bourgeois existentialist or analytical philosophical terms. In response, she develops a bigger picture:

> I have a vision that one of the great gifts that the weaving together of liberation theology and Wesleyan theology can contribute to hegemonic cultures is a discourse of sin that names the reality of suffering and destruction, that criticizes unjust systems in need of correction, and that analyzes basic idolatrous forms of life in need of radical transformation.[7]

In other words, the struggles of women are not merely the problems of individual women but need to be understood as related to the structures of sin. As we engage the pressures of the twenty-first century, both liberation and Wesleyan theologies are well positioned to develop deeper understandings of sin.

It might be argued that from the perspectives of lesbian, gay, bisexual, transgender, queer, and intersex (LGBTQI) communities a deeper understanding of sin is required as well. After all, the main concern of those who oppose even committed same-sex relationships in the church today is related to particular understandings of sin.[8] According to Ted Jennings, a Methodist liberation theologian in the United States, the problem is that sin has often been narrowly understood in terms of sexual issues, blocking

---

7 Rebecca S. Chopp, "Anointed to Preach: Speaking of Sin in the Midst of Grace," in M. Douglas Meeks, ed., *The Portion of the Poor: Good News to the Poor in the Wesleyan Tradition* (Nashville: Kingswood Books, 1995, abbr.: *TPP*), 99.

8 See, for instance, Joerg Rieger, "Is Homosexuality a Sin?" in John Thornburg and Alicia Dean, eds., *Finishing the Journey: Questions and Answers from United Methodists of Conviction* (Dallas: Northaven United Methodist Church, 2000), 11–13.

the broader biblical concern for sin in terms of oppression, injustice, and the biblical concern for the poor.[9] Jennings is right because, particularly in conservative circles where sexuality is often addressed as a problem, the church too often remains silent where sexuality involves sin in blatant forms. Domestic abuse of spouses and children is often covered up, as are other abuses perpetuated particularly by those in power who have their own ways of imposing sexual demands on others.

The topic of sexuality demands that we develop a deeper understanding of sin, understood as a fundamental distortion of relationships that can affect both heterosexual and homosexual relationships. Let's talk about heterosexual relations first. In the United States more women are hurt by members of their own families than by strangers. This distortion of relationship is often overlooked, as fear is usually directed at strangers rather than at relatives. Moroever, this form of sin is often overlooked in churches that tend to forget that the Jesus of the Gospels challenges much of what we call "family values."[10]

Keep in mind that the relationships that Jesus commends above all are not the natural ones among family members but among those who do the will of God. Those are the ones that Jesus calls his "family" in the famous passage in the Gospel of Mark,[11] rather than his physical mother and siblings. To put it bluntly: Jesus never put family before community. In Jesus' model, community is the only context in which families can flourish, and for this reason it appears to be the context in which committed sexual relationships can flourish as well. And while Jesus explicity prohibits abusive relationships—exemplified by divorce, where in antiquity men could dismiss their wives without accountability—he does not prohibit non-abusive relationships whether heterosexual or same-sex.[12]

---

9 Ted W. Jennings Jr., "Breaking Down the Walls of Division: Challenges Facing the People Called Methodist," in Rieger and Vincent, *Methodist and Radical* (abbr.: *MR*), 60.

10 Ibid., 61.

11 Mark 3:31-35.

12 Matt. 19:3-9. It is interesting that even most conservative churches now allow for divorce, even though—unlike same-sex relationships—this is the only thing explicitly prohibited by Jesus.

What is at stake here is more than social ethics; what is at stake is nothing less than "the identity of Christ";[13] that is, the truth of the Christian faith itself. In this context, the deeper theological issue becomes clear. Does this not match the particular critiques of same-sex relations in the Bible? Because committed same-sex relationships were within the purview of the biblical writers, what the remarkably rare passages that mention same-sex relationships reject are abusive relationships where the powerful use others for self-serving pleasure. Once again, sin is understood as distorted relationships. This is especially clear in the Roman Empire, which is the world of the apostle Paul. Here, older men of means sexually used and abused younger men and boys as symbols of their power and might. Putting themselves in the place of God—this is the traditional sin of pride—God "gave them up in the lusts of their hearts to impurity, to the degrading of their bodies among themselves" (Rom. 1:18-32). The problem is theological rather than merely ethical.

Sin, Race, and Ethnicity

Next, let us turn to matters of race and ethnicity. Here, another set of deep theological reflections on sin emerges. Theologian Justo González, a US Hispanic Methodist originally from Cuba, reflecting on matters of ethnicity in conversation with feminist theologians, has pointed out that sin is not always a matter of pride. Although no one may be immune to pride, pride is one form of sin that applies to the powerful in particular, as they are more prone to putting themselves in the place of God due to the structures in which they find themselves. This does not mean that the oppressed and the excluded are free from sin. In this case, however, sin is more likely to manifest as the opposite of pride, in a false humility where people have internalized their oppression and exclusion and thus fail to claim their God-given powers.[14] This is a crucial insight that can emerge only when theology takes into account grace that liberates under pressure

---

13 Jennings, "Breaking Down the Walls of Division," *MR*, 65.

14 Justo González, *Mañana: Christian Theology from a Hispanic Perspective* (Nashville: Abingdon Press, 1990), 137.

and social religion. While sin as pride captures the situation of the powerful who impose pressures on others, sin as false humility and subservience better captures the situation of those who endure these pressures and who are rendered powerless by oppressive structures, including racism and ethnocentrism.

From the perspective of African American theology, Methodist theologian Josiah Young reinforces our understanding that the problem of sin is a deeply theological matter. Racism and the long-standing abuse of African Americans are not merely ethical problems. Wesley himself, Young notes, understood that the abuse of slaves was not simply an offense against moral decency; rather, it constituted an offense against God.[15] And let us not forget that slavery is not just a matter of the past. There are now more people in the world who are held in bondage as slaves, in the literal meaning of the word, than ever before. What is worse, today these slaves have become even more expendable than ever.[16] Racism, defined as prejudice plus power, is still a core factor in these relationships.

Korean American Methodist theologians Andrew Sung Park and the late Jung Young Lee add two important aspects to a broadening understanding of sin. Park notes that in the past we often have been so focused on the salvation of sinners that we have not considered those who are sinned against. Victims of sin do not need a call to repentance, Park says, they need healing. Addressing the victims with a call to repentance makes the situation worse, because it encourages self-hatred.[17] Once again, the definition of sin as pride does not offer the most helpful perspective here. From the perspectives of the victims, Park argues, "we can see the mode of sin more holistically,"[18] thus gaining a broader view of the need for grace that liberates

---

15 Josiah U. Young III, "Distinguishing Sterility from Fecundity in the Wesleyan Tradition," *MR*, 71.

16 In past systems of slavery, slaves were often sizeable investments, thus retaining some value to their masters. See Kevin Bales, *Disposable People: New Slavery in the Global Economy* (Berkeley: University of California Press, 2004).

17 Andrew Sung Park, "Holiness and Healing: An Asian American Voice Shaping the Methodist Traditions," *MR*, 100.

18 Ibid., 96.

under pressure. Of course, this concern for the victims should not mean that the sin of the victimizers can be neglected. Furthermore, I would add, victims need not only healing but also support in order to name the sin they have experienced and to call the victimizers to account so that the vicious circles of victimization will come to an end.

Jung Young Lee looks at the same problem as Park, but from the other side, when he notes that the fundamental Christian problem that needs resolution is what he calls the cardinal sin of centrality. Lee states:

> The church is deeply embedded in centralist motivation. Most are based on a centralist ideology and a hierarchical structure of belief, which both exclude and control the poor, minorities, and the powerless. This is contrary to the essence of Jesus Christ's intent. As Jesus Christ was a marginal person, the norm of the church should be marginality.[19]

We might think of centrality as one of the pervasive forms that the sin of pride takes in our time, not only in the churches but also in the dominant nations of the world, many of which are majority Christian. This matches to some degree the critique of empire put forth by contemporary theologians, including several Methodists.[20] One example of the sin of centrality might be the way churches often deal with poor and less fortunate people. When well-meaning church people try to help others, they often end up trying to turn them into images of themselves. In the process, other identities and cultures are erased.

Native American theologians in the United States have made their own contributions to the topic of sin. Methodist theologian Homer Noley, the author of a Native American theology with two other Native American theologians, George Tinker and Clara Sue Kidwell, defines sin this way:

---

19 Jung Young Lee, *Marginality: The Key to Multicultural Theology* (Minneapolis: Fortress Press, 1995), 123.

20 See Rieger, *Christ and Empire*; Míguez, Rieger, Sung, *Beyond the Spirit of Empire*; see also Ted W. Jennings, "John Wesley," in *Empire and the Christian Tradition*, ed. Kwok Pui-lan, Don Compier, and Joerg Rieger (Minneapolis: Fortress Press, 2007).

> Sin from an Indian perspective can be defined as failure to live up to one's responsibility, sometimes deliberately but more likely as a result of impulsive or unthinking behavior, a mistake. In Christianity, sin has become privatized as a personal matter. For Indian people it is a matter of responsibility to community.[21]

The rediscovery of a communal and structural understanding of the nature and gravity of sin is no small accomplishment at a time when sin is often psychologized or treated as an individual problem.

Note that the insights of other ethnic traditions as well as of the challenges of race do not simply augment mainline theology; these insights add important new impulses, and they contribute to the reshaping of theological understanding as a whole.

Sin and Economic Structures

Latin American liberation theologians are well known for their interpretation of the doctrine of sin in terms of economic structures. Victorio Araya-Guillén, a Methodist theologian from Costa Rica, notes the problem in stark terms: "The dawn of the third millennium confronts us with a painful historical reality of sinfulness: the holocaust of the majority of human beings—the poor of the earth."[22] Here, large numbers of people experience sin in terms of its ultimate consequence, which is death. A common theme of many Latin American liberation theologies is that the poor are the ones who die before their time. While the world has changed since Araya-Guillén wrote these lines in the 1990s, many of the pressures have only grown, and the situation he addresses has not improved but gotten worse. Unfortunately, this kind of sin based in economic exploitation continues to be greeted with silence by much of theology and many churches. Note that efforts to help the poor, such as those witnessed in many churches that are beginning to

21 Clara Sue Kidwell, Homer Noley, George E. "Tink" Tinker, *A Native American Theology* (Maryknoll, NY: Orbis Books 2001), 110.

22 Victorio Araya-Guillén, "The 500th Anniversary of the European Invasion of Abya-Yala: An Ethical and Pastoral Reflection from the Third World," *TPP*, 135.

push beyond ecclesial narcissism, do not yet engage at deeper levels the sinful structures that keep producing and reproducing poverty.

The trademark of the early Latin American liberation theologies was the critique of capitalist ideas of development and the theology that went by that same name, the so-called "theology of development." Argentinean Methodist theologian José Míguez Bonino, in a book that has become one of the all-time classics of Latin American liberation theology, frames the problem in these words:

> Development and underdevelopment are not two independent realities, nor two stages in a continuum but two mutually related processes. . . . Northern development is built on third-world underdevelopment. The basic categories for understanding our history are not development and underdevelopment but domination and dependence.[23]

This critique picks up the insights of the dependency theory, which argues that there is a relationship between wealthier and poorer nations according to which the wealth of some is produced at the expense of the poverty of others. The underlying problem is a theological one, namely sin as the distortion of relationships. Today, this particular distortion of relationships has reached epidemic proportions, and we need to look for the deeper roots of the problem. In addition to the economic relations between the countries of the global North and South, we also need to consider the relations within the North and the South, as there are wealthy and powerful groups in the South and large and growing numbers of exploited people in the North.

The theology of development, like much of liberal theology, missed the stark reality of sin, which is manifested in distorted relationships that have allowed some people to "develop" on the back of others. While liberals tend to be aware of problems with hard imperialism, like the Spanish and Portuguese conquest of Latin America, they are often unware of the problems with soft imperialism, which are tied to efforts at development promoted

23 José Míguez Bonino, *Doing Theology in a Revolutionary Situation* (Philadelphia: Fortress Press, 1975), 16.

by the United States and Northern Europe. This explains the lack of understanding of the imperial implications that accompany even seemingly benevolent efforts of trying to help others. As a result, projects that are supposed to deliver aid and education, for instance, often continue imperial structures under the surface.[24] Grace, in this context, provides development but does not liberate; even if it manages to alleviate some of the symptoms, it perpetuates the problems.

The reality of sin is manifested in the epidemic distortion of relationships and the pressures that are the result.

In the Latin American context, sin has also been defined theologically as idolatry. As Araya-Guillén points out, in agreement with other Latin American liberation theologians, capitalism is a "system of economic idolatry. Idolatry occurs when humankind deposits its faith and life in something that is not God, but a creation of its own hands, the idol."[25] Under the conditions of neoliberal capitalism, the market has become God. Adam Smith's notion of the famous "invisible hand of the market," which supposedly guarantees the success of everyone, exemplifies this problem. Putting something in the place of God that is not God is a consistent theme in Latin American liberation theology.

This concern about idolatry runs parallel to an aspect of the theology of Swiss Reformed theologian Karl Barth that is often neglected in First World theology. According to Barth, the theological struggle is not between faith and atheism or even between faith and the absence of faith. The task of theology is to distinguish between faith and idolatry, good faith and bad faith, as it were. Good faith—might we call this orthodoxy?—is thus a crucial matter in the fight against sin, which can be described as idolatry or heresy, and as we can see under the conditions of neoliberal capitalism, tends to become a matter of life and death for both people and the environment.

24 Much of this happens in the wake of the globalization of the neoliberal economy; see, for instance, Rieger, *No Rising Tide* and Rieger, *Globalization and Theology* (Nashville: Abingdon Press, 2010).

25 Araya-Guillén, "The 500th Anniversary," *TPP*, 139.

This concern for matters of faith corrects a common misunderstanding that liberation theology would be concerned mostly about orthopraxis (right action) and not about orthodoxy. Wesleyan and many other liberation theologians understand that action and faith belong together and reshape each other. Some Methodist theologians have helped to develop this theme further. From a Cuban perspective, Methodist theologian Israel Batista Guerra points out the deceptive qualities of neoliberal economic idolatry, since "the economic influence of the capitalist model [sic] of production is so intrinsically present in Protestantism that it has become a factor of which we are hardly aware."[26] This relation of capitalist action and Christian faith still haunts the Cuban Methodist churches, he says. Examining the churches in the so-called First World in this light leads to similar conclusions.[27]

Further Broadening the Concept of Sin

In addition to a clear sense of sin in its economic form, Latin American theologians have also developed an awareness of sin in a broader framework. Míguez Bonino, for instance, notes that "while oppression may appear dominantly as economic exploitation, or racial discrimination, or political domination, and so on, the other dimensions are also normally put at the service of this dominant organizer of oppression."[28] Such oppression includes personal issues, including psychological structures and people's behavior and emotional makeup. And religion is part of the problem as well, as religion itself becomes sinful when it puts people under all kinds of pressures—psychological ones included—and aids oppression.

Basil Moore, a past general secretary of the University Christian Movement, who was exiled to London and who popularized Black Theology in

---

26 Israel Batista Guerra, "The Missionary Heritage of the Cuban Churches," in *Faith Born in the Struggle for Life: A Rereading of Protestant Faith in Latin America Today*, ed. Dow Kirkpatrick, trans. Lewistine McCoy (Grand Rapids, MI: Wm. B. Eerdmans, 1988), 246.

27 For a broader study of the structures of theology along the lines of economics as religion see Rieger, *No Rising Tide*.

28 José Míguez Bonino, "Methodism and Latin American Liberation Movements," *MR*, 194.

South Africa in the early 1970s, writes about the South African Methodist context. He notes that while South Africans use the title "Black Theology," borrowing James Cone's term, "the content of American Black Theology has not been imported."[29] According to Moore, Black Theology in South Africa brings together issues of sin along the lines of race and class, as it deals with black people "facing the strangling problems of oppression, fear, hunger, and dehumanization."[30] In this approach, the notion of sin is broadened further by taking into consideration what is now called the "intersectionality" of various forms of oppression.[31]

Once again, we need to keep in mind that we are not dealing merely with ethical issues; when we are talking about sin, we are touching the heart of the gospel. In other words, without dealing with sin and the corresponding grace under pressure in particular situations, Christianity is in danger of losing its character.

Cedric Mayson is another white South African theologian who, due to his involvement in the anti-Apartheid struggle, spent time in a high-security South African prison and many years in exile. He talks about the intersectionality of race and class in terms of sin. Quoting a friend, he says: "Because our poor are mostly black and our rich are mostly white, it seems to be a problem of race, but the heart of the problem is the question of wealth and poverty."[32] According to Mayson, the major black liberation organizations in South Africa agree that "the central factor of oppression is economic and people use race as a tool of capitalist oppression and manipulation."[33] Racism, in this context, is a useful tool for economic exclusion, as it allows employers to reject black Africans "whom the white economy does not require."[34] Moreover, racism also becomes a useful tool for playing off whites

29 Basil Moore, "What Is Black Theology?" in *The Challenge of Black Theology in Africa*, ed. Basil Moore (Atlanta: John Knox Press, 1974), 1.

30 Ibid., 6.

31 For the notion of *intersectionality*, see the foundational work of African American scholars Kimberlé Crenshaw and Patricia Hill Collins.

32 Cedric Mayson, *A Certain Sound: The Struggle for Liberation in South Africa* (Maryknoll, NY: Orbis Books, 1985), 38.

33 Ibid.

34 Ibid., 46.

and blacks against each other, privileging lower-class whites over lower-class blacks so that lower-class whites identify with upper-class whites. This stabilizes the upper-class, white-dominated status quo, while lower-class whites benefit much less from their racism than they assume.

However, sin was not merely the problem of South African business leaders and politicians under the conditions of Apartheid. Despite some heroic efforts to resist Apartheid by both communities and individual church leaders like the South African Methodist bishops Peter Storey (white) and Mvume Dandala (black), many churches proved to be a part of the problem. In Mayson's words:

> I have strong feelings about the Security Branch and the Government, but I do not blame them for being hypocrites. It is the leaders of the churches who condone and support this hypocrisy, who recognized the heretical beliefs and continue to accept them, that must bear full responsibility.[35]

In addition, those who look in from the outside are not off the hook either, as they are implicated in sinful structures without knowing it. Again, Mayson says, "People in the West do not know that they are oppressors or part of an oppressive society: they think that they are Liberals and Reformers and do not recognize that these are the garments worn by oppressors."[36] These are strong words, but they bring to light the gravity of sin that is the subject of this chapter. What should be profoundly clear by now is that meaning well is not enough; in fact, meaning well is often part of the problem. As a result, we need to get to the roots of sin. The old saying that "the way to hell is paved with good intentions" may not refer merely to good intentions that are not carried out, as many people believe. We are beginning to understand that there may be something wrong with good intentions as such.

People all over the world share similar experiences of the all-pervasiveness of sin and the pressures that it imposes on people's lives. Korean Minjung theology—*Minjung* meaning "people" or "multitude"—is one example. Korean

---

35 Ibid., 109.

36 Ibid., 138.

Methodist theologian Jong Chun Park, for instance, working in close relation to Minjung theology, has noted the perpetual struggle in which Koreans and other East Asians find themselves: "In East Asia there has never been a time of genuine peace and justice. The Korean minjung has suffered Chinese domination in the old past, Japanese imperialism in the recent past, and American hegemony in the present."[37] This hegemony is another manifestation of the weight of sin, often ignored by theologians and communities of faith.

When viewed in this context, many of the theologies in the First World have produced comparatively weak accounts of sin. Nevertheless, a strong understanding of sin can also be found in the work of Wesleyan liberation theologians in the United States and England. British theologian John Vincent, for instance, has pointed out the Methodist temptation to conform to the cultural establishment and its "embourgeoisement."[38] The problem, we might add, is not whether Methodists are middle or upper class but their efforts to conform to the norms by which these classes function—turning even God into their own image—and a narcissism that refuses to deal with the exploitation of others. Even John Wesley was worried about the Methodists' rise in class status when it led to them forgetting their roots and their solidarity with working people.[39] Sin understood in this way reflects the classical problem of the "*homo incurvatus in se*," the human being turned in on itself that forgets not only about God but also about others—or worse, that seeks to turn others and God into its own image.

It is often forgotten that since the early twentieth century, Methodists in the United State have devised theological critiques of capitalism in terms of sin. Walter Muelder, for instance, Methodist ethicist and former dean of Boston University School of Theology, notes how in 1932, the Social Creed of the Methodist Episcopal Church "radically moved from single-interest reforms to a more systematic examination of the social-economic system." In this context, "the whole capitalistic profit system was addressed. In large numbers church persons and the General Conference asked whether there

37 Jong Chun Park, "Interliving Theology as a Wesleyan Minjung Theology," *MR*, 176.

38 John Vincent, "Basics of Radical Methodism: Challenges for Today," *MR*, 31.

39 See, for instance, John Wesley, "On God's Vineyard," *The Bicentennial Edition of the Works of John Wesley*, 3:515–16.

was not something basically amiss in the industrial and financial order." This broader understanding of sin was not limited to theological statements but was introduced into the practices of everyday ministry and into churches: "A direct responsibility was laid on the local church to investigate local moral and economic conditions as well as to know world needs," notes Muelder.[40]

Rather than merely trying to help—a common approach that tries to cure the symptom without understanding the deeper causes, even today—churches would do well to analyze what sin looks like at present. Of course, addressing sin often encounters pushback, an experience that Jesus as well as John Wesley also had in their own times. The emerging tension is best expressed in the famous words of Brazilian Roman Catholic Bishop Dom Hélder Câmara: "When I give food to the poor, they call me a saint. When I ask why the poor have no food, they call me a communist."[41]

In the aftermath of the 1929 Great Depression in the United States, sin as an economic reality was concretely named and pointed out by many. In 1932 the General Conference of the Methodist Episcopal Church went to the heart of the problem when it declared that "the present industrial order is unchristian, unethical, and antisocial." Also during those years, the Northeast Ohio Conference talked about capitalism as a "pagan economic order" (the term "unchristian" would have been more appropriate because paganism is not the problem), and the Pittsburgh Conference stated that the real problem is capitalism and its "enormous waste . . . its undemocratic control . . . its concentration of wealth."[42] Contemporary debates about what is and is not Christian are almost entirely silent on these topics.

---

40 Walter George Muelder, "The Methodist Social Creed and Ecumenical Ethics," in Ted Runyon, ed., *Wesleyan Theology Today: A Bicentennial Theological Consultation* (Nashville: Kingswood Books, 1985, abbr.: *WTT*), 353.

41 Zildo Rocha, *Helder, O Dom: uma vida que marcou os rumos da Igreja no Brasil* (Sao Paulo: Editora Vozes, 2000), 53.

42 These quotes are from George D. McClain, "Pioneering Social Gospel Radicalism: An Overview of the History of the Methodist Federation for Social Action," in *Perspectives on American Methodism: Interpretive Essays*, ed. Russell E. Richey, Kenneth E. Rowe, Jean Miller-Schmidt (Nashville: Kingswood Books, 1993), 375. In 1934 a survey among five thousand Methodists reported that 39 percent favored replacing

During the Cold War and afterward, state communism in Eastern Europe and Russia was often charged with sinful transgression. In theological studies in the West, the self-critical attitude that is required for detecting one's own sinful state was mostly neglected. Even if most forms of state communism have now collapsed, this does not imply that capitalism is the solution by default. Capitalism, too, needs to be examined in terms of its sinfulness and the pressures that it imposes on people's lives and on the environment. Theological critiques of capitalism have been offered by various Wesleyan theologians; in the United States this group includes J. Douglas Meeks, Ted Jennings, and myself,[43] even though this topic is still not addressed broadly. Surprisingly, the protest of the churches voiced in the aftermath of the Great Depression was missing in the aftermath of what has been called the "Great Recession" in 2007 and 2008. Even today, a response from the churches is still lacking, even though economic conditions for the majority of people in the United States and around the globe have not improved even though the economy recovered.

Pieces of a Bigger Puzzle

As we have seen, there are many significant ways in which Wesleyan liberation theologies have deepened our understanding of sin. The various descriptions are not in competition but can be seen as pieces of a bigger puzzle. As several male Wesleyan theologians have observed, for instance, women often have a better sense of sinfulness than men.[44] This is probably due to the fact that women, even when they hold privileged social positions, are more prone to experiencing oppression than men in similar

---

capitalism with socialism, and 56 percent argued for a "drastically reformed capitalism," (379).

43 See M. Douglas Meeks, *God the Economist: The Doctrine of God and Political Economy* (Minneapolis: Fortress Press, 1989); Ted W. Jennings Jr., *Good News to the Poor: John Wesley's Evangelical Economics* (Nashville: Abingdon Press, 1990); and Rieger, *No Rising Tide*.

44 Vincent, "Liberation Theology in Britain, 1970–1995," 31, also notes the role of women in developing a sense for oppressive situations; Muelder, "The Methodist Social Creed," *WTT*, 355, also notes how the female members of the church were often ahead of the white male members in social matters.

positions. The same might be said of people on the margins more generally as well.

Here are two examples of these epistemological blinders, which show how we tend to be unaware of the structures of sin that surround us. In the early days of my career, when I presented an essay on John Wesley's reversal of top-down and bottom-up religion, I was taken aback that the faculty colleagues at the school where I was teaching seemed unable to grasp the problems with top-down theologies and the need for alternative perspectives. A few days later I presented the same essay to a group of high-school students from some of the poorer neighborhoods. Not only did they understand the point of the reversal immediately, they were able to supply numerous examples from their own everyday experiences.

While workers understand the value of work to a company, management often operates as though the contributions of workers are accidental to the success of a company. Remuneration follows these dominant points of view, as the salaries and benefits of workers are constantly reduced, and salaries and benefits at the top continue to grow. The apostle Paul sensed the deep sinfulness of such top-down relationships when he talked about the body of Christ, telling the head that it must not say to the feet "I have no need of you" (1 Cor. 12:21). As Paul knew so well, "if one member suffers, all suffer together with it" (1 Cor. 12:26).

Yet the point of this chapter is not to dwell on sinfulness; it is to understand the pernicious nature of sin in order to provide deeper understandings of the power of grace that liberates under pressure.

3

Proclaiming Salvation so That It Makes a Difference

Is There Life before Death?

The Wesleyan approach to salvation is much broader than has commonly been realized, and various liberation traditions have been expanding on it further. In his landmark sermon "The Scripture Way of Salvation" (based on Eph. 2:8, "ye are saved through faith" [based on KJV]), John Wesley points out that salvation is primarily to be understood neither as going to heaven after death nor as eternal happiness. Rather, Wesley argues that salvation is what takes place here and now: "ye are saved" or "ye have been saved" is how Wesley translates the passage from Ephesians.[1] The basic focus of salvation in the Wesleyan traditions, therefore, is not on what happens after we die; the basic focus of salvation is on what happens in the present, here and now, as God's grace makes a difference and liberates in the midst of the pressures of life.

Just as sin is the distortion of particular relationships, grace is the restoration of particular relationships, initiated by God.

Salvation is predicated on God's grace. Yet it makes all the difference how we think about grace. In the Wesleyan traditions, grace is not a substance that can be owned like private property; just as sin is the distortion

1 John Wesley, "The Scripture Way of Salvation," in *Works*, 2:156.

of relationship, grace is the restoration of a relationship with God and with other people, a relationship that is initiated by God. Consequently, as I have argued elsewhere: "If grace is what happens in our relationships with God and other people, there is little sense in rehearsing the old question of whether we are talking about an 'otherworldly' or a 'this worldly' process."[2] Neither does it make sense to wonder whether grace refers to a public or a private process or a material or spiritual one, as we shall see. Grace as relationship is all-encompassing, at work whenever God relates to us as individuals or as communities, whether before or after death. This relationship is initiated by God—Wesley called this initiation "prevenient grace"—and it extends to all of humanity, inviting a response.

While Christians are often concerned about whether there is life after death, the Wesleyan notions of grace and salvation invite us first to ask the question of whether there is life before death. Asking the latter question puts the former question on a more solid foundation. If we see that God makes a difference in this life, we have more reason to hope that God will make a difference after we die as well.

If we see that God makes a difference in this life, we can be more hopeful that God will make a difference after we die.

Salvation and grace, therefore, have everything to do with a concern for how we relate to God and to others here and now and what God is doing in and through these relationships. If this is correct, it makes no sense to play spiritual and material matters against each other when we talk about salvation, because our relationship to God and to others incorporates all of reality. Unfortunately, the material qualities of salvation have often been missed in Christian theology. One present-day example is the widespread critique of "consumerism." When preachers and other well-meaning people challenge what they call "consumerism," they often imply that people care too much about "material" things. But what is the alternative? Focusing on immaterial things alone is not an option, as God is at work in the material world. This insight is reinforced by God's incarnation in Jesus Christ as both

2 Rieger, *Grace under Pressure*, 53.

human and God, keeping in mind that the human and the divine are both material and spiritual. A more appropriate critique of consumerism would take into account that, for Christians, there are different ways of relating to the material world. Consumerism is not our only option—God's liberating grace connects us to the material world in more appropriate ways.

In other words, the material and the spiritual belong together, and one informs the other. This is what we mean when we say that grace liberates under pressure. Moreover, there is no need to think of the spiritual and the material as relegated to two mutually exclusive realms, as if the spiritual were otherworldy or immaterial, or as if the material were merely dead matter. Although this has often been forgotten, many of the great revivals of the church, including Methodist ones, were closely tied to social, material, and spiritual empowerment.

Wesley was optimistic, therefore, that God's salvation can make a difference in people's lives and in the world. This optimism has sometimes been described as an optimism of grace. This optimism of grace is not naïve, because Wesley was aware of the structural realities of sin, and he knew the problems and the pressures of life that are often forgotten in churches today. What characterizes Wesley's thinking about salvation is that he was able to find grace at work, not primarily on the mountaintops, where things are easy and success is mostly guaranteed, but on the underside of life, in the unexpected places where many theologians and churches never even look.

Salvation, Sanctification, and Liberation

Míguez Bonino talks about "a christo-soteriologically founded anthropological optimism,"[3] which means that Wesley's optimism about salvation and grace are rooted in what Christ can do in the lives of human beings and their communities. This is the foundation of sanctification in the Wesleyan traditions. In his earlier writings, Míguez Bonino pointed out the limitations

---

3 José Míguez Bonino, "Wesley's Doctrine of Sanctification from a Liberation Perspective," Ted Runyon, ed., *Sanctification and Liberation: Liberation Theologies in Light of the Wesleyan Tradition* (Nashville: Abingdon Press, 1981, abbr.: *SL*), 61.

of Wesley's notion of sanctification, which had to do with being focused too much on the individual and with a related failure to critique the dominant status quo. This, he noted, led Methodists "to accept their role in society and to improve their lot without challenging the rules of the game."[4] Nevertheless, Míguez Bonino later acknowledged that there are other ways to read Wesley's doctrine of sanctification and that Wesley had more to say in regard to the communal and, therefore, the political and economic aspects of sanctification.

Another Latin American Methodist theologian, Elsa Tamez, adds to this insight, noting that Wesley's notion of sanctification can be described broadly as "the struggle for life"; she even identifies a parallel to Roman Catholic theologian and poet Ernesto Cardenal's notion of the "holiness of revolution."[5] We must never forget that in the Wesleyan tradition, sanctification is one significant way in which God's salvation is at work in a fundamental transformation of the world.

Sanctification does not mean accommodating to the dominant status quo—a common misunderstanding by Wesleyans who want to be part of the dominant culture. Sanctification does not mean to live up to the norms and regulations of the status quo, including common definitions of "decency" or "normalcy"; rather, sanctification means organizing alternative ways of life according to the will of God and joining in God's liberation of the people and the world from the structures of sin.

In 1977 Ted Runyon, a Methodist theologian in the United States, summarized a growing congruence between sanctification and social change in his introduction to an influential volume on the topic of "Sanctification and Liberation." He notes:

> There is a peculiar affinity between Wesleyan theology—especially Wesley's doctrine of sanctification—and movements for social change. When Christian perfection becomes the goal of the individual, a fundamental hope is engendered that the future can

4 Ibid., 59.

5 Elsa Tamez, "Wesley as Read by the Poor," in *The Future of the Methodist Theological Traditions*, ed. M. Douglas Meeks (Nashville: Abingdon Press, 1985), 82.

> surpass the present. Concomitantly, a holy dissatisfaction is aroused with regard to any present state of affairs—a dissatisfaction that supplies the critical edge necessary to keep the process of individual transformation moving.[6]

We should add that this holy dissatisfaction works on both the personal and the social levels because Wesley does not limit the kingdom of God to the life of individuals or to life after death. Recall Wesley's definition of the purpose of Methodism: "To reform the nation, particularly the Church; and to spread scriptural holiness over the land."[7] Once again, religion is always social religion for Wesley.

Salvation and the Work of God

Salvation in the Wesleyan tradition begins with the work of God, and this is reflected in many liberation theologies, which are keenly aware that oppressed people cannot pull themselves up by their own bootstraps (an impossibility, upheld by those in power to blame others).

In feminist theology, for instance, there are strands that pick up this emphasis on the work of God in connection with the relation to God and neighbor. In the words of US Methodist theologian Rebecca Chopp: "It is only through hearing the word of God and neighbor that radical transformation, including the emancipatory transformation of changing oppressive social systems and unjust economic systems, occurs."[8] This emphasis on salvation grounded in listening to God and neighbor is in agreement with Wesley that salvation needs to be focused on transformation that takes place here and now. Chopp notes that "a Wesleyan feminist theology can offer a way of Christianity by combining the feminist insistence on Christian praxis of emancipatory transformation with Wesley's notion of Christianity as a way

6 Ted Runyon, "Introduction: Wesley and the Theologies of Liberation," *SL*, 10.

7 John Wesley, "Minutes of Several Conversations between the Rev. Mr. Wesley and Others," *Works* (Jackson), 8:299.

8 Rebecca S. Chopp, "Hearing, Holiness, and Happiness: Listening to God and Neighbor," *MR*, 119.

of love of God and neighbor."[9] In other words, the transformation toward which feminists work is not merely a political issue, as emancipatory transformation is deeply woven into the salvific ways of the love of God in the world.

An emphasis on the work of God in salvation is common in other liberation theologies as well. Black Theology in the United States, for instance, has given expression to it in the words of renowned Methodist theologian James Cone. Salvation, according to Cone, "is a divine action that embraces the whole world, changing our relationship with God and making us new creatures."[10] This emphasis on the work of God has consequences, because it focuses not primarily on the preferences of Christians and their churches—or on their perceived needs—but on the preferences of God. This emphasis on the work of God is the context in which we need to understand the following statement by Cone:

> The Christian view of reconciliation has nothing to do with black people being nice to white people as if the gospel demands that we ignore their insults and their humiliating presence. It does not mean discussing with whites what it means to be black or going to white gatherings and displaying what whites call an understanding attitude.[11]

There can be no reconciliation without liberation, which means setting people free from the structures of sin that distort every aspect of their lives, which in this case is the sin of racism. This further broadens our conversation about grace that liberates under pressure. Cone's summary leaves no doubt about the centrality of liberation in the work of God, which defines what salvation means for the world: "Christ is the Reconciler because he is first the Liberator."[12]

---

9 Ibid., 112.

10 James H. Cone, *God of the Oppressed* (New York: The Seabury Press, 1975), 228.

11 Ibid., 226–27.

12 Ibid., 230. Cone also says: "White people must be made to realize that reconciliation is a costly experience. It is not holding hands and singing 'Black and white together' and 'We shall overcome.' Reconciliation means death, and only those who are prepared to die in the struggle for freedom will experience new life with God." Ibid., 239.

From a Korean American perspective, Andrew Sung Park follows up on his assessment that the doctrine of sin needs to take into account the wounded with a focus on the particular shape of the work of God: "God achieves the healing of the sinned-against and the sanctification of the sinner in the process of synergetic healing. By setting the wounded free from their oppression, the Spirit heals their wounds." As God initiates a healing process, the victims of sin are liberated from what oppressed them and are empowered to collaborate with God. Here, the emphasis on the work of God opens out to a perspective that includes the work of the redeemed human being in liberation: "Graced by the Holy Spirit, the wounded can confront and transform the *han* of the world with their own wounds."[13] *Han* is a Korean term that connotes suffering, sin, and evil. Healing and liberation thus include confrontation of sin, as the healing of wounds does not imply a cover-up of sin but a way of overcoming it.

"Christ is the Reconciler because he is first the Liberator." —James Cone

Salvation, Community, and Politics

Native American theologians in the United States, including Methodist Homer Noley, have emphasized the communal aspect of salvation that has often been lost in the history of Western theology and even in some interpretations of Wesley. For Native Americans, say Native American theologians Tinker, Noley, and Kidwell, "salvation can be defined as the ability of an individual or a community to return to a state of *communitas* that has been disrupted."[14] This is an important insight that further broadens our theological horizons of salvation, and it is closely related to the ways in which many traditions in the Bible talk about salvation in terms of community. Particularly in the Hebrew Bible, salvation was never considered as related only to individuals or to the private property of individuals; rather,

13 Andrew Sung Park, "Holiness and Healing," *MR*, 106.

14 Kidwell, Noley, and Tinker, *A Native American Theology*, 110.

salvation was aimed at the well-being of the whole community, manifest in the covenants with Abraham, Noah, and Moses.

No matter what our various theologies have to say about salvation, it can never be confined to individual or personal issues. Even when theologies tried to confine salvation in this way by focusing on life after death, there were consequences for the bigger picture, because these positions often endorsed the ecclesial, political, and economic status quo without being aware of it. Not challenging the powers that be usually means endorsing them. Even those who define salvation as individual holiness in this life, which includes many of the current heirs of the holiness traditions in Methodism and Pentecostalism, tend to fall into the same trap, because they ignore the powers that be, not realizing how they shape us all the way to the core.

In other words, when theology and the church refuse to deal with the broader implications of salvation for politics, this does not mean that politics disappears or loses its influence on our lives. The opposite is the case: when political (and economic) powers are ignored, they tend to return under cover, through the back door as it were. German Methodism had to learn this the hard way; even though most German Methodist churches did not openly support the politics of Nazi Germany during the era of the Third Reich, by not addressing the topic and by not mounting opposition they inadvertently became part of the problem. Whether we like it or not, grace that liberates under pressure has political consequences.

What does it mean for Wesleyans to "reform the nation" when grace has political consequences?

From the Latin American perspective, Míguez Bonino has raised the following question, which has deep implications for the doctrine of salvation: "Can Methodism be understood as an attempt to 'reform the nation,' or is it to be seen as religious accompanying music to the introduction of industrial capital?"[15] The latter option was, of course, the fate of many of the

15 Míguez Bonino, "Salvation as the Work of the Trinity: An Attempt at a Holistic Understanding from a Latin American Perspective," in M. Douglas Meeks, ed.,

early Methodist efforts in Latin America. There, it was particularly Methodism's efforts to promote education that supported the capitalist expansions into Latin America that mushroomed at the time, although Methodists were mostly unaware that they supported the status quo in this way. When Methodists built schools in Latin America, for instance, they would have had the opportunity to contribute to strengthen local communities and transform the local situations had they understood these structures. Without understanding the political and economic situation, however, they often ended up preparing people for service to the dominant business ventures of the day, many of them headquartered in the United States.

For Míguez Bonino, the question is whether Methodists can participate in a "genuine Latin American project of social transformation."[16] How would we answer that question today in terms of what theology and churches are doing on the ground and how they are shaping and reshaping communities not only in Latin America but elsewhere as well? How does our Wesleyan understanding of sanctification contribute ways of life that push beyond the established status quo of our communities and our politics?

Reconciliation and the Reality of Salvation

Salvation and grace, in this context, need to be understood as concrete realities, described and defined in terms of what they accomplish in the midst of sin—the pressures and tensions that large groups of people experience. Míguez Bonino discusses the notion of reconciliation in this way, starting with the biblical concept:

> Reconciliation is not achieved by some sort of compromise between the new and the old but through the defeat of the old and the victory of the new age. The ideological appropriation of the Christian doctrine of reconciliation by the liberal capitalist

---

Trinity, Community, and Power: Mapping Trajectories in Wesleyan Theology (Nashville: Kingswood Books, 2000, abbr.: *TCP*), 69.

16 Ibid.

> system in order to conceal the brutal fact of class and imperialist exploitation and conflict is one—if not the—major heresy of our time.[17]

There is a parallel to Cone's critique of reconciliation, cited above, as salvation must not refer to a reconciliation that covers up, ignores, or even endorses clear forms of injustice, be they matters of race, class, or gender. The work of salvation is to address injustice wherever it is found and overcome it; it cannot lend itself to tolerance of, or compromise with, sin and evil. This can be seen in the ministry of Jesus, who did not preach reconciliation without a challenge, denouncing Herod and the Pharisees who made common cause with the status quo of the Roman Empire. Refusing to compromise with them, he nevertheless continued to love them.[18] Rather than a premature embrace or premature reconciliation, salvation and grace at times amount to tough love. This is another example of grace that liberates under pressure.

Salvation and grace . . . need to be understood as concrete realities, described and defined in terms of what they accomplish in the midst of sin.

Any understanding of salvation as reality in this life needs to include the cross of Christ, including the suffering and pain that go with it. The Uruguayan Methodist theologian Julio de Santa Ana reminds us that "human life must pass via the cross. Only thus, without triumphalism, and recognizing that we cannot avoid either suffering or pain, can we confront the powers of this world, the true counter powers of Jesus Christ."[19] Here, suffering and pain can take on a positive function in the resistance to sin. Salvation can never be a triumphalist concept that works from the top down, without getting anyone's hands dirty. In the liturgical year of the church, there can be no Easter without Good Friday. The two always belong together, reshaping each other for the sake of liberation.

---

17 Míguez Bonino, *Doing Theology in a Revolutionary Situation*, 121.

18 Ibid., 121–22.

19 Julio de Santa Ana, *Good News to the Poor: The Challenge of the Poor in the History of the Church*, trans. Helen Whittle (Maryknoll, NY: Orbis Books 1979), 108.

While many of the concepts of liberation theology work well in a Wesleyan framework, some concerns emerge as well. One example is the notion of the unity of history, which has been critiqued by Wesleyan liberation theologians. The unity of history was a key concept in Roman Catholic liberation theology in Latin America, designed to overcome conservative attempts at splitting history in two parts, one sacred and the other secular. This split led to a neglect not only of what was happening in the world and in the church but also of what God was doing in both parts. The unity of history, bringing the church, the world and God back together again, was, therefore, an important theological affirmation. Míguez Bonino speaks on behalf of others, however, when he cautions not to take this unity of history too far. Clearly, a strong split of sacred and secular is problematic because the history of the world and the history of the church can never be neatly separated, as there are too many overlaps, and because God cannot be divided. Nevertheless, Míguez Bonino explains, "for us Gentile Christians to confess the Kingdom is not only to enter into the meaning of our own history but also to take distance from it and to be grafted into another history."[20] In other words, the unity of history has its limits, because God's actions in history cannot be equated directly with human actions.[21] By the same token, encounters with Christ can never be equated directly with encounters with the poor.[22]

In South Africa, after the end of Apartheid, the broadening understanding of salvation had to be rethought. Charles Villa-Vicencio, a Methodist South African theologian who held key leadership positions in the South African Truth and Reconciliation Commission, has given an account of the

---

20 Míguez Bonino, "Salvation as the Work of the Trinity," *TCP*, 77.

21 This was one of the main concerns of US liberation theologian Frederick Herzog, who, though not a Methodist, spend most of his career teaching at the United Methodist-related Duke Divinity School. See, for instance, his lengthy introduction to the English translation of Latin American liberation theologian Hugo Assmann's book *Theology for a Nomad Church*, trans. Paul Burns, preface by Frederick Herzog (Maryknoll, NY: Orbis Books, 1975).

22 Míguez Bonino, "Salvation as the Work of the Trinity," *TCP*, 78. This is an important concern for Methodist liberation theologians. I have dealt with this problem in my book *Remember the Poor*.

different theological challenges during and after Apartheid in South Africa. Even after the end of Apartheid, he notes, it is still necessary to deal with the socioeconomic order inherited from the past. The goal must be the "transformation of the existing order to the benefit of the poor."[23] Villa-Vicencio points out what he considers to be a parallel to recent Latin American liberation theology, which also has shifted "from the systematic resistance of the past to nuanced reconstruction in the present."[24] We must keep in mind that the cause of the poor is promoted, not by the clash of ideas, but in actual struggles on the ground,[25] and any effort at reconciliation needs to take this into account so as not to glance over real conflict. Grace that liberates under pressure must always be linked to the actual struggles of people, and it demands specific accounts of what difference is being made.

Grace that liberates under pressure must be linked to actual struggles.

While Christian theologians like to talk about reconciliation, the topic can be highly problematic, especially in situations of great power differentials. The idea of reconciliation has too often been employed to tell the oppressed to forgive and forget, while those who benefit from systems of oppression may feel contrition but continue with business as usual. I vividly recall a long conversation with a black South African Christian in 2008, who kept insisting that his task was to forgive all whites without any need to hold them accountable to the past and without any commitment on their part

23 Charles Villa-Vicencio, "Freedom Is Forever Unfinished: The Incomplete Theological Agenda," in *Being the Church in South Africa Today: Papers Delivered at the Consultation on South Africa in Regional and Global Context: Being the Church Today*, eds. Barney N. Pityana and Charles Villa-Vicencio (Johannesburg: South African Council of Churches, 1995), 59.

24 Villa-Vicencio, "Freedom Is Forever Unfinished," 62.

25 Ibid., 63–64. Villa-Vicencio seeks to push beyond capitalism and socialism. But perhaps at the time he underestimated the power of capitalism, although he notes the importance to build alternatives to exploitative capitalism, which is the place where the old and the new agendas of liberation are connected (ibid., 69).

to transformation. What real work is grace doing in this situation if it is not allowed to contribute to the pursuit of transformation and liberation of both the oppressed and the oppressors?

Former South African Methodist presiding bishop Mvume Dandala notes the problem with such shallow ideas of reconciliation and poses a deeper challenge for the doctrine of salvation:

> The crucial question is whether the developed world can be persuaded to harness its appetite for the resources of the developing world in order to allow processes to emerge that enable all to benefit from these resources without eroding our ecology and environment. . . . This may be our evangelical challenge.[26]

Once again, this is another powerful reminder that there can be no reconciliation without transformation; salvation is incomplete otherwise, and the evangelical challenge is neglected.

North American Methodist theologian Mary Elizabeth Moore talks about repentance and reparation in conjunction, both being notions that have deep implications for a more profound understanding of reconciliation. Moore begins by noting that *repentance* includes a "special privilege of voice granted to the oppressed, underrepresented, or marginalized." *Reparation*, in this context, pertains to "the concrete repairing of injuries and relationships." What comes to mind, though not mentioned by Moore, is the story of Zacchaeus, who restores fourfold what he had taken (Luke 19:1-10). No easy reconciliation is possible, notes Moore, "because reconciliation is not a place to rest."[27] Grace can become concrete through reconciliation when the perpetual challenge of reconciliation is understood and embodied.

---

26 H. Mvume Dandala, "Methodist Mission to Ecological Challenges in Africa," in M. Douglas Meeks, ed., *Wesleyan Perspectives on the New Creation* (Maryknoll, NY: Kingswood Books, 2004, abbr.: *WP*), 113–16.

27 Mary Elizabeth Mullino Moore, "New Creation: Repentance, Reparation, and Reconciliation," *WP*, 113–16.

Participating in Salvation

In the Wesleyan traditions, salvation—the work of God in the lives of humanity and the world—is inextricably linked with people working alongside God. As Korean Minjung theologian Jong Chun Park has pointed out: "The famous Wesleyan doctrine of assurance in relation to the witness of the Spirit tends to become enthusiastic if it is disconnected from another Wesleyan doctrine, that of faith working through love."[28] This is a reminder that Christianity needs to be grounded in the real difference that grace makes in situations of pressure; without this grounding, it can become a dangerous illusion that ends up supporting the status quo without being aware of it.

In the British context, John Vincent notes the importance of following Christ in the context of the doctrine of salvation: "The heart of religion was the imitation of Christ. To be perfect was to be perfectly like Christ, filled with 'love divine.'"[29] This is a reminder that, from the perspective of liberation theologies, there is a close relation between the work of God and the work of Christians. In Wesley's own theology, the work of God is not conceived in narrowly religious terms, so he noted the parallel of works of piety and works of mercy, realizing that the latter are real means of grace as well.

Works of mercy and solidarity are channels through which we invite and receive God's grace into our lives.

If, as I point out in my book *Grace under Pressure*, works of mercy are indeed means of grace, the point is not that those who act mercifully earn salvation. The opposite is the case: works of mercy (today we might call them works of justice and solidarity, as Wesley's ministry went beyond what we today call charity), like works of piety (reading the Bible, praying, and taking Holy Communion), are channels through which we invite and receive God's grace into our lives, and through which we are empowered to follow God's work in the world.[30] This changes everything.

28 Park, "Interliving Theology," *MR*, 172.

29 Vincent, "Basics of Radical Methodism, *MR*, 36.

30 On this topic see Rieger, *Grace under Pressure*, ch. 2.

Hence, what has often been considered as social activism and thus merely a secondary ethical application of the heart of Christianity, now moves front and center and becomes an essential part of salvation and grace. Salvation, understood as God's gracious action in the lives of humanity and the world, focuses on what God is doing in the world and what we are called to do in response, rather than on the performance of our individual piety and its rewards. This reversal is crucial, and it seems that, in contemporary theology, liberation theologians are the ones who have understood this most genuinely and profoundly. Here, Wesleyan theology still has a good deal of work to do, because not understanding these dynamics jeopardizes the Methodist movement as a whole.

Wesley himself cautioned us about this when he warned that even Methodists who performed all the works of piety could fall from grace if they did not realize that works of mercy were also means of grace.[31] Imagine: Wesley assumed that Methodists who went to church every Sunday, who prayed and read the Bible every day, were in danger of falling from grace! In a different context, it was Dietrich Bonhoeffer who understood that the church can be the church only if it is the church for others. In the words of North American Methodist theologian Ted Jennings: "In visiting the marginalized we invite them to transform us, to transform our hearts, to transform our understanding, to transform us into instruments of the divine mercy and justice."[32] Here, relationship is crucial once again, and grace that liberates under pressure opens up into a two-way street, coming full circle.

In sum, the common question of whether there is life after death can be answered in the affirmative only if we can show that there is indeed life worth living before death, that grace does its work of liberation not only after we have died but also before, not only in individual lives but also in the community and in the world. In other words, if there is no real life before death, we might need to caution people about trusting statements that affirm life after death.

---

31 See John Wesley, "On Visiting the Sick," in *Works*, 3:385.

32 Jennings, *Good News to the Poor*, 57–58.

4

Reenvisioning God, Church, and the Bible

God

The doctrine of God is arguably the singular and most important battleground for theology today. The default definition of God is similar in many non-liberation theologies: God is somehow found at the top. According to Anselm of Canterbury, God is that than which nothing greater can be thought. Thus, God's power is envisioned in categories that reflect this location at the top. Some more conservative theologies might think of God in terms of a monarch or an individual strong leader who exercises unilateral power from the top down. Other models related to this outlook include some versions of the Intelligent Design argument, where there is an entity that designs and also controls everything from a central location (or at least did design and control everything in the past).

Liberal theologies are less severe, even though some of their models of God still tend to operate from the top down. Here, God might be thought of in terms of a social entrepreneur or reformer who is in control of a project, perhaps resembling the power of an elected official who, once in office, works from the top down. Other liberal theologies think of God in less hierarchical terms—perhaps working from within or as a foundation—but rarely do we encounter radical reversals of the top-down model. Despite these differences, where liberals and conservatives often agree is when they talk about leadership: God's leadership is envisioned as operating from a place of superiority, like a choreographer, an advocate, the head of a multinational company, or the head of a powerful megachurch. Even when less anthropomorphic images of God are used, there still is a tendency to think of God in terms of a supreme power or a higher power, located above everything else.

This is not fundamentally different from the theism espoused in the days of the Roman Empire, which is the context in which early Christianity developed. Here the various gods, including the Roman emperor, who was envisioned as God, ruled in hierarchical fashion from the top down. The early Christians were considered atheists by the Romans, not because they did not believe in a god, but because their God did not conform to this dominant hierarchical order. Jesus Christ being put to death on a Roman cross and associating with common people introduced a very different tone into the Christian understanding of God.

Unfortunately, many theologians today fail to understand that we cannot have it both ways. Even when theologians are trying to incorporate alternative images into their doctrines of God that are less hierarchical, top-down images of God tend to linger on, sometimes below the surface, and they shape our theologies unless they are addressed. In addition, it makes no real difference whether this top-down power is envisioned in terms of hard power, embodied, for instance, by authoritarian rule with an iron fist and coercion and violence, or soft power that proceeds through enticement, persuasion based on privilege, and the manipulation of people's desires.

Liberation theologies open the door for envisioning God differently.

Liberation theologies have opened the door for envisioning God differently, thus reclaiming some of the insights of early Christianity that have often been lost in contemporary Christianity, Methodism included. The various liberation theologies share in common an understanding that God's power is not found at the top but at the bottom. This does not mean that God would give up power. God does not "divest" Godself of power, as some well-meaning liberals insist. Divesting oneself of power is never a good idea, neither for God nor for people, as this leads to awkward vacuums of power, where the privileged seek to abdicate their privilege and romanticize the situation of people on the margins. Yet there is never a vacuum of power, as dominant power moves in where power is not reclaimed.

Rather than creating artificial vacuums of power, liberation theologies hold that God deconstructs dominant power and reconstructs it in alternative ways. This deconstruction and reconstruction is deeply rooted in the Christian traditions, most clearly visible in the incarnation of God in Christ, which is often understood as *kenosis*, self-emptying, according to Philippians 2:7, and reclaiming power in this way. In the final temptation in the Gospel of Matthew (4:1-11), Jesus rejects the devil's offer to give him top-down power over all the empires of this world, once again deconstructing and rejecting dominant power. Of course, this temptation would not amount to much if Jesus merely rejected the devil's offer of hierarchical power, expecting that God would give him precisely this kind of power a short time later. In rejecting the devil's offer of top-down power, Jesus rejects hierarchical power once and for all, testifying to the fact that God's power is radically different (Matt. 4:8-10). Power is both deconstructed and reconstructed in Jesus' life, ministry, death, and resurrection.

This reconstruction of power can be observed in various places in the Bible as well as in the later traditions of Christianity. The Nicene Creed teaches us an important lesson in this regard. When the emperor Constantine called the Council of Nicaea in 325 CE and presided over it, it looks as if he found a way to to domesticate the church's beliefs about Jesus by putting Jesus on the same level as God, who was commonly assumed to wield top-down power like the emperor. There is, however, another way to interpret the Nicene Creed. If Jesus is indeed of the same substance as God, and thus fully God, as the Creed states, this can mean two very different things. For the Roman Empire, it meant that Jesus was now incorporated into a dominant theism, according to which God, by definition, is impassible, immutable, and omnipotent. As a result, this Jesus lost the identity of his radical life and ministry. Alternatively, the Nicene Creed does not prevent us from interpreting the reality of God in terms of the the life and ministry of Jesus Christ, fully human and divine. This perspective reshapes our images of God as being at work, not from the top down, but working in solidarity with the people, suffering with them, and struggling for justice with them.

Many conservatives and liberals fail to understand the challenge embodied in the Nicene Creed, as conservatives are often stuck with dominant theistic ideas about God (like emperor Constantine); and liberals tend to downplay the equality of Jesus with God, preferring to see Jesus as a great prophet, activist, or role model. Unfortunately, by giving up the notion that Jesus is of the same substance as God, liberals also give up the opportunity to reconstruct core images of God.[1]

The core concern of a theology that investigates liberating grace under pressure has to do with the doctrine and character of God. After all, it is God who initiates the work that saves us from sin and who liberates, and it makes all the difference whether this God is at work from the top down or whether God's power manifests itself in different ways. In this sense, liberation theologies are not primarily about social ethics but about more profound understandings of God. As John Vincent and I have stated in an edited volume titled *Methodist and Radical*: "None of this will mean anything unless God in Christ through the Holy Spirit is the first radical."[2]

Liberation theologies are not primarily about social ethics but about more profound understandings of God.

Ted Jennings appears to be in agreement and notes the deeper reasons for Wesley's ministry, which are too often neglected in mainline Methodism: "We often recall that Wesley directed himself to the poor of England and away from the prosperous and prestigious." The reason for this was "the rigorous application in the field of proclamation and community formation of the biblical revelation of the being of God."[3] Wesley's reason for focusing the Methodist movement on the poor and marginalized, on

1 For the complete background of this account see Joerg Rieger, *Christ and Empire*.

2 Joerg Rieger and John Vincent, "Conclusion," *MR*, 207–8.

3 Ted W. Jennings, "Transcendence, Justice, and Mercy: Toward a (Wesleyan) Reconceptualization of God," *RWT*, 82. Jennings, reflecting on Psalm 82 and Exodus 3, states even more strongly: "The being of God is constituted as a relationship to the violated and humiliated," this is what "distinguishes the God of the Bible from all other gods" (ibid., 65).

liberating grace under pressure, has to do first of all with his understanding of God and not with practical or political deliberations; Wesley is not merely engaging in what is now called "needs-based ministry." This is absolutely fundamental to understanding the Wesleyan tradition and to any subsequent Methodist theology. Douglas Meeks agrees in his own way: "The concentration of Wesley's view of stewardship on the poor is not an ideological quirk. It derives from the character of the God of Israel."[4] The core issue for the church as it engages the challenges of our time needs to be a robust doctrine of God.

When trying to understand God in terms of grace that liberates under pressure, some of the generic attributes of God are challenged and reshaped. When liberation theologians talk about God taking sides, for instance, mainline theology is shaken in its foundations. Is not God supposed to be on everyone's side or at least neutral? African American liberation theologian James Cone has been known to make strong claims, such as the following: "From God's side, reconciliation between blacks and whites means that God is unquestionably on the side of the oppressed blacks struggling for justice."[5] Yet this claim, which appears harsh at first sight, matches the logic of the Bible, which Wesley sought to apply in his own context. God in Christ is found on the side of those who are experiencing the pressures of life, pushing back against those who are comfortable and inflict burdens on others, as the Gospels testify. Some "tie up heavy burdens, hard to bear, and lay them on the shoulders of others" (Matt. 23:4), but Jesus defies them, devising a different way of life: "My yoke is easy, and my burden is light" (Matt. 11:30).

Cone further notes that "God encounters evil and suffering, the principalities and the powers that hold people in captivity; and the resurrection is the sign that these powers have been decisively defeated, even though they are still very active in the world."[6] We might add that the God who makes a difference is a God who takes the sides of those who are oppressed

---

4 M. Douglas Meeks, "Sanctification and Economy: A Wesleyan Perspective on Stewardship," *RWT*, 87.

5 Cone, *God of the Oppressed*, 235.

6 Ibid., 236.

and exploited ("blessed are you who are poor," Luke 6:20) and challenges those who oppress and exploit ("woe to you who are rich," Luke 6:24), as the ministry of Jesus demonstrates.

In his work with Salvadoran immigrants in the United States, North American Latino Methodist theologian Harold Recinos reports that "radical discipleship . . . included nothing less than confronting the established church's theological view of God ruling in almighty power and trampling the poor." Here, Recinos also learned about the alternative, "a genuine surrender to the God of compassion who favors trampled people."[7] God's power is not disputed here, but it is reconstructed in terms of acts of compassion and of resistance against sin and evil.

Those in power who uphold the status quo are not forgotten, but their priorities have to be reordered, which implies a challenge. In Jesus' own words: "The last will be first, and the first will be last" (Matt. 20:16). Might this be the reason why it is often so difficult to speak about such biblical images of God in well-to-do churches? Why is there such resistance to conversations that push beyond status-quo images of God?

When Roman Catholic liberation theology in Latin America formulated its famous "preferential option for the poor" in the late 1960s, the theological foundation was not some naïve idea of the goodness of the poor but a theological sense of the goodness of God, who cares about "the least of these" (Matt. 25:45). At stake are not romantic views of the poor but the question of the character of God, which might be described as love tempered by justice. At the heart of Latin American liberation theology is precisely this kind of love, an issue on which Catholics and Wesleyans can agree. As Míguez Bonino notes: "The 'option for the poor' is simply the concrete sign of the universality and intentionality of love."[8] This universal love is rooted in the love of God, which is not an empty universal idea but which takes the sides of the oppressed and calls the oppressors to accountability.

Of course, God loves everybody, but this love takes different shapes and forms, including what we today might call "tough love." This issue has deep

---

7 Harold J. Recinos, "Barrio Christianity and American Methodism," *MR*, 79, 80.

8 José Míguez Bonino, "Wesley in Latin America: A Theological and Historical Reflection," *RWT*, 179.

roots in the Wesleyan traditions. Ted Jennings is one among others who has identified a preferential option for the poor in Wesley's own work.[9]

Néstor Míguez, a Methodist theologian and biblical scholar from Argentina and a liberation theologian of the current generation, reclaims the horizons of liberation theology in the nonrevolutionary situation of contemporary empire (recall that his father, Míguez Bonino, wrote about theology in a revolutionary situation). The new creation, Míguez proclaims, now as then, has to do with "God's saving judgment for the poor, the despised, and the excluded," pointing to an alternative way of life. Today however, he notes, we are clearer than ever before that this new creation is God's and not ours, because we have run up against the limits of what humans can do.[10] Focusing more clearly on the work of God is what sustains the hope of Christians so that the cause of the marginalized is not lost, even when revolution does not appear to be as imminent as it once did. This matches what we have called Wesley's optimism of grace in the previous chapter. Without a clear commitment to God and God's work from the bottom up, theology tends to become part of the status quo.

Without a clear commitment to God's work from the bottom up, theology tends to become part of the status quo.

The Wesleyan traditions have always been most powerful and meaningful precisely where they found God at work outside of the spectrum defined by the theological status quo. Wesley himself anticipated this when he insisted that religion must not go from the greatest to the least (see chapter 1). His lifelong concern for the least of these is therefore not merely a matter of social awareness or ethical commitment but a theological

---

9 Jennings, *Good News to the Poor*, ch. 3.

10 Néstor Míguez, "The Old Creation in the New, the New Creation in the Old," *WP*, 69. Míguez describes the challenge of the empire thus. Under the conditions of empire, public matters are subordinated to private interests, "the democratic republican political ethos of the nation-state is substituted by the power of private benefit through corporate action" (ibid., 57).

one. Many Methodists found God in places where mainline religion least expected it, often outside the church in the fields and the streets, among working people, the sick, and the imprisoned. While mainline Methodism moved away from this soon after Wesley's death, other Wesleyan traditions continued this sensitivity.[11]

The good news is that the Wesleyan traditions still have some important contributions to make in this search for God as the one who acts in surprising and challenging ways and continues to push us beyond our comfort zones. This is our Wesleyan legacy, at the heart of our particular understandings of sin, salvation, and grace, but we still need to grasp the meaning of this insight more deeply and profoundly. As Ted Jennings has argued, this is one of the places where John Wesley himself, while possessing the right theological instincts, did not go far enough. No theologian, no matter how brilliant, will ever be able to comprehend the divine altogether, and this is why we need to continue this task today and why we have to work in community. This brings us to the doctrine of the church.

Church

The Wesleyan understanding of the church has always been complex. For most of his life Wesley saw no need to split off the Methodist movement from the Anglican traditions, and his doctrine of the church does not differ significantly from Anglicanism. More important, however, is the fact that when Wesley talks about the church, he talks about it as a movement with a particular history that has particular accomplishments and shortcomings, and not as an abstract entity that can be defined without attention to its life. For Wesley, the measuring stick of a Christian, and thus of the church, is "that whole mind, all those tempers, which were also in Christ Jesus."[12] From this point of view, the Methodist understanding of the church is deceptively simple: the church is a community of people who live in accordance to God in the world, in the midst of what we have called liberating grace that is at

---

11 See, for instance, Stephen Hatcher, "The Radicalism of Primitive Methodism," *MR*, 123–37.

12 John Wesley, "On God's Vineyard," *Works*, 3:508.

work under pressure. Ultimately, it is only in that dynamic situation of the Christian life that any liberation theology make sense, as these theologies are not the products of individuals but, in good Methodist fashion, grow out of the life of particular communities of faith that embody the character of God in the world. This understanding of the church leaves no room for the ecclesial narcissisms that have become so widespread today.

The famous Latin American Bishop's Conferences, in Medellín, Columbia and Puebla, Mexico in 1968 and 1979, exemplify similar dynamics in the Roman Catholic Church. Here the church took a close look at the life of its communities, expressed in powerful ways in the so-called Base Ecclesial Communities, which consist of small groups of Christians who read the Bible in the context of their everyday struggles and who hold one another accountable, much as the early Methodists did. In this context the preferential option for the poor developed, growing out of popular readings of the Bible, not as an ideological commitment but as lived efforts to bring the church closer to the reality of God. It was based on these grassroots developments that the Roman Catholic Church in Latin America embraced its commitment to the poor—and it should give us pause that subsequent challenges to this approach came mostly from the top, including Rome.[13]

In South Africa, the famous Kairos document of 1985 exemplifies a similar dynamic. Here ecumenical church groups came together to affirm central concerns of liberation in the context of Apartheid. Methodist theologians were an integral part and played important roles in the writing of the document. The Kairos document talks about "prophetic theology," not as an abstract concept, but as something that grows out of particular communities that seek to follow God for the benefit of the world. Such theology has to take sides, as God "does not attempt to reconcile Moses and Pharaoh," but "takes sides with the oppressed" because "oppression is sin and cannot

13 These challenges included not only investigations that at times resembled the old Inquisition (located in the same office, now renamed the "Congregation for the Doctrine of the Faith") but a consistent effort by Rome to replace the generally progressive bishops in Latin America with conservative ones.

be compromised with."[14] Once again, the basic character of the church is not based on an ideology; it is based on a growing awareness of the work of God, moving from the bottom up rather than the top down. Over the years there have been many other statements made by Methodists along similar lines, many of which can be found in the *Book of Resolutions* of The United Methodist Church. In the United States the African Methodist Episcopal Church published a statement in 1976, titled "Liberation Movements: A Critical Assessment and a Reaffirmation," which talked about the inextricable relation of the church and liberation in theological terms, rooted in the particular history of the black church.[15]

Unfortunately, many of these ecclesial traditions are overlooked or even forgotten in Methodism today. One reason is a sharp but ultimately problematic theological distinction between what is considered binding theological essence and what is considered negotiable social application. In The United Methodist Church, for instance, the so-called Social Principles that speak about the social commitments of the church are not considered binding in the same way that doctrinal statements are, like the Wesleyan Articles of Religion or the Confession of Faith.[16] Apart from the fact that the Social Principles are rarely used in worship, such a sharp distinction between social creeds and religious creeds is faulty for various reasons. First, in Wesley's own thinking, as expressed, for instance, in the General Rules, which (unlike the Social Principles or the Social Creed) are part of the binding constitutional documents for United Methodism, there is no sharp distinction between theological essence and social application. Wesley considered as binding for Methodists not only

---

14 The Kairos document, in Charles Villa-Vicencio, *Between Christ and Caesar: Classic and Contemporary Texts on Church and State* (Cape Town: David Philip, 1986), 263.

15 Position Paper of the AME Church, in *Black Theology: A Documentary History*, eds. James H. Cone and Gayraud S. Wilmore, vol. 1: 1966/1979, 2nd rev. ed. (Maryknoll, NY: Orbis Books, 1993), 250–56. On page 254, the following statement is made: "The liberation movement had its origin in the formation of the Black Church. Much of the post-Emancipation leadership for the liberation movement came from the Black Church."

16 The preface to the Social Principles in the *Book of Discipline* states that the Social Principles are "not to be considered church law"; they are merely "intended to be instructive and persuasive." *Discipline* (2012), 103.

doctrinal statements but all three parts of the General Rules, "doing no harm," "doing good," and "attending upon all the ordinances of God."[17]

As pointed out above, works of mercy and works of piety can never be separated in Wesleyan theology, and this sense is deeply anchored in our constitutional General Rules. Moreover, it is not possible to identify a sharp distinction between theological essence and social application in the life and work of Jesus (read Matthew 25:31-46), and not even Paul draws such a line, as recent research has shown.[18] Perhaps we should consider this distinction between the theological and the social a modern heresy that is more closely tied to the Enlightenment's definition of religion as non-political and private than to the traditions of Christianity.

The 1996 United Methodist Bishops' Initiative on Children and Poverty helps us deepen our understanding of church along the lines of grace liberating under pressure. In this initiative, the bishops of the global United Methodist Church examined the pressures endured by children in poverty from a theological perspective. Their conclusion is that the church does not primarily need more social programs:

> The crisis among children and the impoverished and our theological and historical mandates demand more than additional programs or emphases. Nothing less than the reshaping of The United Methodist Church in response to the God who is among "the least of these" is required.[19]

This is a strong claim, and Douglas Meeks notes the theological challenge: "Who is God in the face of children in poverty? Who are we *coram deo* (before God) in the face of children in poverty?" This is the Wesleyan way of doing

17 John Wesley, "The Nature, Design, and General Rules of Our United Societies," in *Discipline* (2012), 75–78.

18 See, for instance, Richard Horsley, ed., *Paul and Empire: Religion and Power in Roman Imperial Society* (Harrisburg, PA: Trinity Press International, 1997), and John Dominic Crossan and Jonathan Reed, *In Search of Paul: How Jesus's Apostle Opposed Rome's Empire with God's Kingdom* (New York: HarperSanFrancisco, 2004).

19 The Council of Bishops of The United Methodist Church, *Children and Poverty: An Episcopal Initiative* (Nashville: The United Methodist Publishing House, 1996), 7.

theology, Meeks explains, wondering, "Why is there no Methodist revival for the survival of children?"[20] The answer lies in our failure to understand that engagement with the world and the least of these is at the very heart of our existence as Methodists and as Christians. One thing is clear: the church cannot produce its own reality, and we cannot be the church without refocusing on God and God's concern for others, both inside and outside of the church. This is why religion is always social religion, as pointed out in the beginning of this book. This insight provides some hope for the church, but also a dire warning.

The deeper problem of the church is best seen from outside the power centers of the Western and Northern churches. Methodist theologian Mercy Amba Oduyoye, from Ghana, talks about a fundamental inequality at the heart of the church: "A cultural and religious domination continues to exist in the relationship between the Northern churches and their Southern counterparts that thwarts any hope for mutuality and partnership."[21] This relation of domination between the North and the South, Oduyoye observes, is sadly mirrored in the relation of men and women in African communities, where religion can be a powerful form of control. Oduyoye's observation applies also to the relation between the status quo and the margins in the churches of the Northern hemisphere. The alternative would be partnerships in mission and mutuality in service, which grow out of an awareness of what Oduyoye calls the "hazards of life," or what we are calling the pressures of life. She concludes with an important question to the church that still remains to be answered: "What is the African contribution to the North?"[22]

In more general terms: What is the contribution of churches in the South to churches in the North? The answer might be found in Oduyoye's description of how Methodists in Ghana have embraced both Wesleyan concerns for healing and deliverance of individuals from evil, as well as a deep concern for the social evils of our time. The good news is that grace is at work

---

20 M. Douglas Meeks, "Trinity, Community, and Power," *TCP*, 18.

21 Mercy Amba Oduyoye, "The Challenges of Partnership and Mutuality in the Task of Evangelizing Ghana," *MR*, 156.

22 Ibid., 157, 162.

in these situations and is making a difference. In sum, Wesleyan liberation theologies encourage rethinking and rebuilding the church from situations of liberating grace under pressure at the margins, where God is at work.

Mortimer Arias, a former bishop of the Evangelical Methodist Church in Bolivia, and his wife Esther remind us of the importance of evangelization in Latin America liberation theology as a holistic endeavor:

> When [the Latin American Bishops' Conference in] Puebla elaborates on evangelization, we Protestants—who are so committed to evangelization and consider it our fundamental vocation—would do well to listen. The Puebla interpretation of evangelization is thoroughly holistic, in the context of the Gospel, in the scope of evangelization (to evangelize the poor, the elite, youth, the family, the church, culture, popular religiosity, etc.) and in the methodology of evangelization.[23]

Evangelization is a central theme for a theology that explores liberating grace under pressure, as it defines the character of the church, and it is too often forgotten that Roman Catholic liberation theologians like Gustavo Gutiérrez have declared evangelization the primary purpose of liberation theology. Put even more pointedly, the question of evangelization can be considered to be the fundamental question of the Christian life. In the words of José Míguez Bonino, evangelization asks the question, "What does it mean concretely and specifically to follow Christ in thought and action in today's world?"[24] Following Christ in public—this is what the church is ultimately all about. This is the place of word, sacrament, order, and service—and all the other activities of the church.

We do not bring the Gospel to the poor. The poor bring us into the Gospel.

23 Esther and Mortimer Arias, *The Cry of My People: Out of Captivity in Latin America* (New York: Friendship Press, 1980), 119.

24 Jose Míguez Bonino, "Sanctification: A Latin American Rereading," in *Born in the Struggle for Life: A Rereading of Protestant Faith in Latin America Today*, ed. Dow Kirkpatrick, trans. Lewistine McCoy (Grand Rapids, MI: Wm. B. Eerdmans, 1988), 13.

Keep in mind also that in situations where people truly experience liberating grace under pressure, evangelization cuts both ways. John Vincent talks about his experience of being evangelized by the poor: "The practitioner theologian does not 'bring' the Gospel, but is rather brought into the Gospel, or aspects of it, through the experiences of the poor, and the experiences of working with them."[25] This changes everything; and it can be argued that John Wesley himself was able to be such a powerful witness to the gospel, because he not only evangelized others but experienced this evangelization by others as well. This is powerfully expressed in one of the hymns of his brother Charles that, unfortunately, cannot be found in any hymnal:

> We still the old objection hear,
> Have any of the great, or wise,
> The men of name and character
> Believed on Him the vulgar prize?
> Our Saviour, by the rich unknown,
> Is worshipped by the poor alone.
> The poor, we joyfully confess
> His followers and disciples still,
> His friends, and chosen witnesses,
> Who know His name, and do His will,
> Who suffer for our Master's cause,
> And only glory in His cross.[26]

Asian Methodist theologians who have suggested the importance of interreligious dialogue have picked up an important Wesleyan theme without naming it, further broadening our understanding of the church. It is well known that John Wesley collaborated with Christians of other

---

25 John Vincent, "A New Theology and Spirituality," in *Liberation Spirituality*, ed. John Vincent and Chris Rowland, British Liberation Theology 2 (Sheffield: Urban Theology Unit, 1999), 100.

26 Published in *The Poetical Works of John and Charles Wesley*, ed. G. Osborn (London: Wesleyan-Methodist Conference Office, 1871), 11:411–12.

denominations on the basis of joining the common cause of loving others.[27] What is less understood is that engaging in this common cause also transforms how we deal with interreligious encounters.[28] Korean Methodist theologian Jong Chun Park, for instance, has argued that interreligious dialogue happens in the crises and pressures of life. In the context of a Christian-Confucion dialogue—both religions struggle with patriarchal components—Park lifts up

> the groans and moans of the most oppressed and marginalized in East Asia, such as women, migrant workers, children, and the so-called lesser in society, as well as all suffering sentient beings in one of the most polluted regions of the world.[29]

Paying attention to these struggles is not just a matter of decency or social engagement; it changes the way people of faith engage in interreligious dialogue in fundamental ways.

Interreligious dialogue that is built on common practices of love, embodying grace under pressure, changes how we build the church in positive ways, because we are beginning to realize that the church cannot and does not need to be built in isolation, by itself. As Christian faith is working in love (Gal. 5:6), collaborating with other religions in situations of pressure does not have to mean giving up one's religious identity; rather, it means becoming more aware of one's own theological motivations at a deeper level and better understanding of what contributions our particular faith in God can make. In the process we become able to listen to others

---

27 John Wesley, "Letter to A Roman Catholic," *Works* (Jackson), 10:85: "If we cannot as yet think alike in all things, at least we may love alike. Herein we cannot possibly do amiss. For of one point none can doubt a moment,—"God is love; and he that dwelleth in love, dwelleth in God, and God in him."

28 While Wesley did not develop this thought, probably because there was no practical way of collaborating with other religions in his context, keep in mind that he had positive things to say about Native Americans, for instance, because they, unlike the Europeans, understood how to live simply and not to "lay up for yourselves treasures upon the earth" (John Wesley, "Upon Our Lord's Sermon on the Mount: Discourse the Eight," *Works*, 1:616–17).

29 Park, "Interliving Theology," *WP*, 124.

and to learn from them about how their particular faiths in God make a difference, just as others can learn from us.

Bible

Wesleyans in general hold to the primacy of scripture, even when they claim the so-called Methodist quadrilateral of scripture, tradition, experience, and reason. But what does professing the primacy of scripture really mean? Some people seem to think that the authority of the Bible is a matter of percentages: Should it have 50, 80, or 100 percent of authority? A better question might be what actual difference the Bible makes in our lives. Does the Bible have the power to shape us, and if so, in what ways? And what difference does the Bible make in situations of conflict and pressure, when other forces compete for our attention?

When reflecting on the authority of the Bible, I often ask people to give examples of how it has shaped their own lives instead of telling me what authority they think the Bible should have. In my own life, for instance, my reading of the Bible is ultimately what compels me to do the work that I am doing as a Methodist liberation theologian in the Wesleyan tradition. Instead of dealing with other, more prestigious and lucrative topics, such as religion and science (I do have a physics background), I have been working on topics of oppression, exploitation, exclusion, and liberation for three decades. Taking seriously the authority of the Bible compels me to keep looking for God's grace in situations of pressure and tension, to deepen my solidarity with those whom Jesus calls "the least of these," and to raise the sometimes uncomfortable topics that I am addressing in this book.

The Bible is most authoritative when it makes a real difference in our lives and communities . . . not when it is put on a pedestal.

The Bible is most authoritative when it makes a real difference in our lives and communities, pushing beyond the ecclesial status quo, not when it is put on a pedestal with grand proclamations about its authority. The

Bible is not to be worshiped in the place of God; it is not God, but it points to God, especially when it is read in the midst of the tensions of life.

A concern for what difference the Bible makes in our lives is at the heart of both Wesleyan and liberation theologies. For the most part, liberation theologies have their origins in communal readings of the biblical texts. The Latin American Base Ecclesial Communities are perhaps the most well-known example. But Black Theology in the United States derives from a reading of the Bible as well, in light of the collective African American experience. The theologian, according to James Cone, is "*before all else* an exegete, simultaneously of Scripture and of existence." In this context the Bible is "the primary source of theological discourse."[30] This may come as a surprise to some, but liberation theologians in the Wesleyan tradition have been more outspoken about the primacy of scripture than many other Wesleyan theologians. This emphasis on the primacy of scripture is not merely an idea of theologians like Cone and others, and is not merely an ideal, as it often is in certain conservative efforts to uphold the authority of scripture without much consideration of what difference it makes in situations of pressure.[31]

Moreover, the primacy of scripture, as affirmed by Black Theology has a centuries-old tradition: it is rooted in slave religion. The slaves understood the liberating powers of the gospel based on their own encounters with the biblical texts, which is why their masters made sure that the slaves would not read the Bible without guidance. The liberating grace under pressure that the slaves experienced came from their own encounters with the stories of the Bible, often shared and further developed in secret meetings and personal conversations. What was preached to them by their white masters or by the established churches was, of course, also taken from the Bible; however, the message was for the most part not about liberating grace but about submitting and being obedient.[32]

---

30 Cone, *God of the Oppressed*, 8, emphasis in original.

31 Conservative emphasis on the virgin birth of Jesus, for instance, rarely tells us what difference this makes in the pressures of real life.

32 For a popular but fairly accurate depiction of this difference, see for instance the recent movie "Birth of a Nation" (2016).

In the South African situation, Methodist biblical scholar Itumeleng Mosala has picked up on the importance of the Bible in his own way, noting the tensions within scripture itself that can be used in support of various different projects. "A black biblical hermeneutics of liberation must battle to recover precisely that history and those origins of struggle in the text and engage them anew in the service of ongoing human struggles."[33] Once again, the Bible plays its most important role, not when it is put on a pedestal, but when it is read in the midst of the tensions of life, where the liberating powers of the text as well as the dangers of oppressive readings and texts become manifest and can be negotiated.

In Latin American liberation theology, as already indicated, the primacy of scripture is rooted in the practice of Ecclesial Base Communities that read the Bible in light of their everyday struggles. Here, rather than in the methods of political theory or in abstract revolutionary ideals, are the roots of Latin American liberation theology. For good reasons Roman Catholic theologian Gustavo Gutiérrez has talked about the fact that Christians not only read the Bible; the Bible also "reads us."[34] In Hispanic theology in the United States, Methodist theologian Justo González has made similar comments, noting that "the [biblical] text that we address addresses us in return."[35] It is no coincidence that this insight is also implied in the Wesleyan understanding of the Bible as a means of grace, through which God reaches into our lives by empowering the text to shape us.[36]

Latin American biblical scholar Elsa Tamez picks up on this tradition and notes that throughout history some Methodists have continued the time-honored Wesleyan practice of reading the Bible from the perspective of the poor.[37] This is what Tamez has done in her own way throughout her career,

---

33 Itumeleng J. Mosala, *Biblical Hermeneutics and Black Theology in South Africa* (Grand Rapids, MI: Wm. B. Eerdmans, 1989), 20.

34 Gustavo Gutiérrez, *We Drink from Our Own Wells: The Spiritual Journey of a People*, foreword by Henri Nouwen, trans. Matthew J. O'Connell (Maryknoll, NY: Orbis, and Melbourne, Autralia: Dove, 1984), 34.

35 González, *Mañana*, 86.

36 For more on this topic see Rieger, *Grace under Pressure: Negotiating the Heart of the Methodist Traditions*, 82–85.

37 Tamez, "Wesley as Read by the Poor," 72.

thus producing important insights into fundamental theological topics. One of them is a significant reinterpretation and deeper understanding of Paul's notion of justification by faith from the perspectives of the struggles of Latin Americans.[38]

From the South African perspective, Basil Moore sums up what happens when scripture is read in the real-life situation of people under pressure in South Africa. Moore notes that this does not mean that liberation theologians can do with the sources whatever they want—just the opposite. Rather than reading the Bible in self-serving ways—which often happens when the Bible is read in abstraction from real life—reading the Bible in situations of pressure has brought us closer to the original issues addressed by the biblical authors who were themselves experiencing the pressures of their times. We should not forget the fact that much of the Hebrew Bible is linked to the impression of various empires, starting with Egypt, and that the entire New Testament was produced under the conditions of the Roman Empire. After all, Jesus himself "was one of the poor, the colonized, the oppressed."[39]

Reading the Bible in contexts of tension, which in many ways resemble the tensions of the times when these texts were written, leads to deeper exegetical insights, which are usually more profound than the ones produced in the ivory towers and other places of comfort. Moreover, it can be argued that these readings tend to be more authoritative in the sense that they actually transform people's lives and move them forward in often surprising ways. That is what grace under pressure looks like.

Oduyoye notes the irony implied in the different uses of the Bible. Methodism in Ghana began with a few young men reading the Bible, but when "the Bible study group called for Bibles," they did not only get more Bibles but "missionaries in addition" to make sure that the Bible was read in certain

---

38 Elsa Tamez, *The Amnesty of Grace: Justification by Faith from a Latin American Perspective*, trans. Sharon Ringe (Nashville: Abingdon, 1993). One of her key insights is that "insofar as it is by faith and not by law that one is justified, the excluded person becomes aware of being a historical subject and not an object" (ibid., 166).

39 Moore, "What Is Black Theology?" 8.

ways.[40] The unfortunate truth is that the readings of the Bible by the people in situations of pressure have too often been policed by mainline theology and its various accommodations to the status quo. Where these dynamics were successfully challenged, the readings of the Bible from the perspective of the people who experience the pressures of life not only led to new theological insights but also made a difference in both the church and the world.

The point, then, is that today we are once again encountering profound respect for the Bible and fresh ways of thinking about authority. The respect of which I am talking differs from the sort of respect that renders things unapproachable and removes them from the touch of real life. Putting the Bible on a pedestal and out of reach, and thus preventing people from offering their own interpretations, is the wrong sort of respect. This is so, not only because it keeps people from reading the Bible in the midst of pressure, but also because it prevents people from truly engaging the Bible and thus being transformed by it.

When I was a student in seminary, I found myself engaging the Bible less and less, not because I had lost respect for the Bible, but because I had developed the wrong sort of respect. In the rarefied world of the German academy, the Bible appeared to be so high above everyday life and ordinary minds that only experts were allowed to deal with it and interpret it, and only their opinions mattered when a decision about an interpretation had to be made.

Reading the Bible in the pressures of everyday life implies another kind of respect and unleashes its authority with new force.

Bringing the Bible back into the pressures of everyday life, reading it there and expecting people to be able to learn from it and interpret it so that it makes a difference, implies another kind of respect and unleashes the authority of the Bible with new force. This does not mean that the academy or the work of professional theologians is without value, but it needs to be embedded in the experience of grace under pressure.

40 Oduyoye, "The Challenges of Partnership and Mutuality," *MR,* 153.

5

Conclusions: Deep Solidarity

The theologies that were introduced in these chapters share the Wesleyan concern to take seriously grace that liberates under pressure not only in the church but also in the world, not only in private but also in public. They provide fresh visions for how the Wesleyan traditions can engage us in constructive fashion, as they are not copying the dominant theological methods of the past and the present, whether they come under liberal, conservative, or other banners. While people have always taken the differences between liberation theologies and conservative theologies for granted, there are also significant differences that separate liberation theologies and liberal theologies, as I have shown throughout these chapters.

This is especially important in the United States, where liberalism is one of the dominant traditions and where even conservatives endorse traditionally liberal ideas; for instance in their staunch support of neoliberal capitalism and its ongoing quest for deregulation and the freedom of capital. Moreover, the policies of development have spread liberalism far beyond the United States and Europe. In some places, like Latin America, liberalism has a long tradition as well, beginning with the early nineteenth century, after various countries declared their independence from Spain's and Portugal's more conservative ways.

When challenged from the margins and from grace that liberates under pressure, liberals and conservatives often find themselves on the side of the status quo and join forces. Míguez Bonino describes the Latin American situation in these words: "When, since the end of World War I, the masses entered public life, conservatives and liberals became more and more unified around the defense of the capitalist order." As a result, "Roman Catholicism and Protestantism could, after a long war, join hands in the support of a democratic, enlightened, liberal society in Latin America."[1] Whenever the poor and marginalized appeared on the map, liberals and conservatives moved closer, and the most pressing theological differences were quickly settled. Similar dynamics can be observed in many other contexts as well, even when the political fight between liberals and conservatives still appears to be in full swing.[2] In contemporary academic and ecclesial settings in the United States and in Europe, for instance, different theologies, which may not share much else in common, tend to find themselves united in their aversion for liberation theologies.

In this context, those of us who seek to take seriously grace that liberates under pressure have little choice but to continue moving toward "a total overhaul of Christian piety, ecclesiastical institutions, discipline, and theological reflection," as Míguez Bonino already put it in the 1970s.[3] This echoes the call of the Protestant Reformation, to which the Wesleyan traditions owe a certain debt of gratitude, that a reformed church must keep reforming itself. To be sure, this is no easy task, but it is well under way, despite many attacks and attempts to declare concerns for liberating grace and corresponding liberation theologies as matters of the past. Until the life-threatening pressures produced by the structures of sin die out, the need for grace that liberates under pressure will not have come to an end.

One common critique, and perhaps the most pernicious of all misunderstandings, is that liberation theologies are special-interest theologies, geared toward the interest of particular minority groups, with no relevance for others. While I have addressed this reproach in detail in other places, a

---

1 Míguez Bonino, *Doing Theology*, 13.

2 While there are significant differences between liberals and conservatives in the United States today, both have in common their support by big money and their proclivity to subordinate their policies to it.

3 Míguez Bonino, *Doing Theology*, xxiv. In Latin America, this was especially important in Protestant contexts. Míguez Bonino notes that among Protestants in Latin America, theological reflection is a new effort. For the longest time, they used translations and adapted European or North American theology (ibid., 73).

few words need to be said in response.[4] Theology, whether it is aware of it or not, has always been contextual; theology, no matter how much it may think of itself as universal, has always addressed particular interests. Since there is no universal point of view—how could there be, as humans are finite and limited?—the theologies that used to consider themselves to be universal turn out to be merely universalizing their own particular perspectives. Once this is clear—most people who have ever come in touch with their own limits know this intuitively—relativity is unavoidable in any theological enterprise. But once we acknowledge our relativity, we can think about how to deal with it. Acknowledging our relativity does not have to lead to relativism, where "anything goes." In any case, denying relativity will not help us overcome relativism, but dealing with it might.

Liberation theologies can help us overcome relativism, and the same is true for Wesleyan theologies that follow Wesley's example of solidarity with the impoverished, the sick, and the imprisoned. Rather than being special-interest theologies, I would argue that these kinds of theologies are common-interest theologies, because common interest is better developed from the bottom than from the top. Efforts to define common interest from the top have not managed to defeat relativity. Such efforts usually take their starting point in universal notions of humanity and human experience, as exemplified by modern European and American theologians like Rudolf Bultmann and Paul Tillich, as well as in the early work of some feminist theologians like Rosemary Radford Ruether, who claimed a generic "women's experience." Every time this happened, however, particular experiences were universalized—like the experiences of white middle-class German men or white American women—ending again in special-interest theologies that got stuck in their own relativism without knowing it.

Liberation theologies are not suggesting universal experiences or a universal context. Like the theology of John Wesley, they pay attention instead to the lives of people who actually experience grace under pressure, including people marginalized along the lines of race, ethnicity, class, gender, and

4 See, for instance, Joerg Rieger, "Developing a Common Interest Theology from the Underside," in *Liberating the Future: God, Mammon, and Theology*, ed. Joerg Rieger (Minneapolis: Fortress Press, 1998), 124–41.

sexuality. Initially, there was some mutual suspicion among the representations of these various perspectives, and even today the various points of view do not always find themselves in agreement. Nevertheless, we are also beginning to understand that the various different contexts are related in certain ways. The context of the poor, for instance, is inextricably related to the context of the wealthy (Wesley, unlike many contemporary Wesleyans, was aware of this), which means that paying attention to the poor does not endorse relativism but an understanding of how everyone is related. The context of women, to give another example, is inextricably related to the context of men; the context of Asians is related to the context of Europeans, Americans, and so on.

The challenge before us, therefore, is to go to the bottom of our contexts, where we can see the various relationships that exist between us, in both their positive and negative shapes. The apostle Paul knew this well when he noted in his comments on the church as the body of Christ that "if one member suffers, all suffer together with it; if one member is honored, all rejoice together with it" (1 Cor. 12:26). Some labor unions seem to have taken Paul more seriously than many churches in this matter, expressed in the motto that "an injury to one is an injury to all." In one of my early essays on this topic I concluded, therefore, that "context is that which hurts."[5] And since Paul spoke these words about the body of Christ, theologians could do worse than looking for God in these places of common pressure, struggle, and joy. Here, acknowledging our relativity under pressure can help us find the path to the common good and overcome relativism.

In a few of my recent publications, I have suggested the term "deep solidarity,"[6] dealing with some of the complications of the notion of solidarity. Too often, people of faith confuse solidarity with advocacy, which usually means that the privileged put themselves on the side of the underprivileged and become their voice, speaking out for them. This has created

---

5 Joerg Rieger, *Liberating the Future*, 127–33.

6 Joerg Rieger and Kwok Pui-lan, *Occupy Religion: Theology of the Multitude* (Lanham, MD: Rowman and Littlefield, 2012). See also Joerg Rieger and Rosemarie Henkel-Rieger, *Unified We Are a Force: How Faith and Labor Can Overcome America's Inequalities* (St. Louis: Chalice Press, 2016).

several problems, including a patronizing attitude by those who think of themselves as privileged, and a neglect of the agency and voice of those who are thought to be on the receiving end. Deep solidarity serves as a reminder that more of us are in the same boat than we realize, which is to say that many more of us are in need of grace that liberates under pressure. In this context advocacy is not enough, even though it is an improvement over charity that addresses the symptoms of problems but not their roots.[7]

In the days of the Occupy Wall Street movement there was a conversation about the difference between the 99 percent and the 1 percent, meaning that as many as 99 percent of the population are less and less—and some not at all—benefiting from the neoliberal economic system. Even the middle class in the United States is experiencing some pressures, although in less severe forms. At stake is not just money but, more important, power. In the current system it is the 1 percent (and really the 0.1 percent) who have the power to make things happen and to change things. This is most visible at the macro level of a globalizing economy, but this power reaches into everything, including national governments and local churches. In this scenario, middle-class Christians are part of the 99 percent rather than the 1 percent, and even in privileged settings like the United States the middle class needs to understand that its power and influence is fairly limited. Middle class people need to learn that they are not able to make things happen on their own without the solidarity of those for whom they are trying to speak out and with whom they seek to be in solidarity.

Wesleyans of the middle class need to understand that solidarity with the 99 percent is not just a lofty ideal but a reality, as they, too, are under attack, facing increasing uncertainty of employment, including underemployment and unemployment, potential loss of benefits at work and in retirement. This becomes even more visible when middle-class people look at their relationships: The future of their children

Deep solidarity means that we have more in common than meets the eye and that we cannot flourish without one another.

7 For a discussion of the differences between charity, advocacy, and deep solidarity, see Rieger and Henkel-Rieger, *Unified We Are a Force*, ch. 3.

is increasingly undecided, as many young people of the middle class are unemployed and move back home after college, unable to make ends meet. The future of their parents is increasingly undecided as well, as they may become dependent on their children, since their benefits may not be sufficient and their investments are insecure. Unless middle-class people acknowledge at least some of the more severe pressures they face in their own lives, they cannot enter into solidarity with anyone else, and certainly not with the proverbial "least of these" to which Wesley and the early Methodists were drawn.

Deep solidarity means, therefore, that we have more in common than meets the eye and that we cannot flourish without one another. This insight allows grace to become active in new ways, as we become more fully aware of God's presence with those who suffer and struggle under great pressure. This awareness of the presence of God—at the heart of both liberation and Wesleyan theologies—is the theological basis of deep solidarity. Of course, this does not mean that we are now all the same and that the differences between us have all disappeared. There is an obvious difference, for instance, between middle-class families who still have decent housing and many others whose housing is found wanting, including homeless families who are forced to sleep under bridges and on park benches. There is a difference between white males who benefit both from racial and gender privilege and women who belong to ethnic minority groups.

Deep solidarity does not imply that we forget about our differences; the opposite is the case: deep solidarity enables us to find ways to make use of our differences for the common good. And deep solidarity reminds us that those who experience the greatest pressures in their own bodies and who are thus closest to experiencing grace under pressure have something to teach the rest of us and need to be part of whatever leadership emerges.

Middle-class persons, for example, who understand that they are more closely connected to working-class persons than to the ultra rich can now use their limited economic privilege for the common good. Working-class men who understand that they are more closely connected to working-class women than to their male employers can now use their limited male privilege for the common good. The same is true for white workers who understand that they have more in common with black workers than with white management.

Of course, the 1 percent are not excluded from these dynamics, but they need to make sincere and sustained efforts to put themselves in solidarity with the 99 percent—the biblical figure of Zacchaeus (Luke 19:1-10) being an example—lest they exclude themselves. Neither Jesus nor Wesley ever gave up on the 1 percent but called them to join the movement; only a few followed the call, but the ones who did were able to make a difference.

Grace comes alive in the midst of the pressures that we experience, not as a uniform thing—grace is never "one size fits all"—but in the form of new relationships with one another and with God. Grace is what makes deep solidarity happen, and grace values difference, enabling people to make use of their struggles and of their limited privileges for the common good. This is what happened in the days of the Jesus movement and in the early days of the Wesleyan movement, and this is what can happen again in the church and other social movements.

Grace is never "one size fits all"; it comes to life in the midst of the pressures that we experience.

Today, some of this is happening again where movements are forming to combat injustices such as racism, sexism, and class exploitation; and churches in the Methodist and Wesleyan traditions need to make sure that they are not missing the boat. Recall that at one point Methodists were part of the causes for the abolition of slavery, support for working people that brought us the forty-hour workweek and benefits, and the Civil Rights Movement. In all these cases, religion was social religion, establishing the kinds of vibrant relations with other people and with God that appear to be lacking in much of what churches are doing today.

Is God on our side, or are we on God's side?

Based on this history it is therefore not unrealistic to hope that Wesleyans can once again become part of the new relationships that God is forming in the world. Keep in mind, however, that these relationships and the emerging deep solidarity that goes with them require us to take sides. This is the nature of grace that liberates under pressure, and if we fail to choose sides, our sides will be chosen for us. Too often, Methodists have assumed that God would be on our side by default. Yet only when we position ourselves on the side of God can we say with John Wesley that "the best of all is God is with us." May the grace of God that liberates under pressure be with us all.

6

"Naked to Follow the Naked Christ"

Imitation of Christ and Solidarity in Wesleyan Ecclesiology

José Carlos de Souza

As this title suggests, there is an indissoluble link in John Wesley's theology between soteriology and ecclesiology, both of which frequently appear in tension, if not opposition, especially after the Reformation. There is no doubt that soteriology was a key element in Wesley's theology. The call to discipleship or, in Wesley's terminology, to the imitation of Christ was its evidence. Likewise, the expression "naked to follow the naked Christ" appears, in Latin, in Wesley's Journal entry for March 7, 1736, as he was beginning his ministry in Savannah, Georgia. One of the readings suggested by the lectionary for that Sunday was the well-known 1 Corinthians 13, which became the text for Wesley's sermon. However, he connected it to Luke 18:29-30, in which, according to his interpretation, Jesus foretold the fate he and his followers would meet.

> In the Second Lesson, Luke 18, was our Lord's prediction of the treatment which he himself (and consequently his followers), was to meet with from the world and his gracious promise for those that are content, *nudi nudum Christum sequi*: "Verily I say unto you, there is no man that hath left house, or friends, or brethren, or wife, or children, for the kingdom of God's sake, which shall not receive

manifold more in this present time, and in the world to come everlasting life."[1]

Based on this account, we can legitimately conjecture about the disposition guiding Wesley's pastoral work in the New World. If, in other circumstances, John Wesley had declared his desire to seek his own salvation and that of others, perfecting himself in the path of holiness, he now shows himself ready to pursue his intent to the end: to strip and empty himself, to abandon all securities whether false or true—it matters not—and to fully bare himself for Christ's sake. For Wesley, it seemed to be the only way to follow the One that had nowhere to lay his head. And Wesley was signaling his willingness to pay the price necessary to be recognized as a disciple of Jesus: "naked to follow the naked Christ." It is certain that Wesley never gave up the idea that the Christian life irrevocably implies taking up the cross, stripping oneself of everything that might prevent following Christ.[2]

However, what is the relationship between the radical demands for Christian discipleship and our ecclesial life together as implied in the terms *koinonia* and *solidarity*? At first glance we find none, at least as Protestantism typically understands this question. Indeed, it has become commonplace to maintain that ecclesiology is the "Achilles' heel" of evangelical theological reflection. By emphasizing salvation by grace alone, Luther, at the beginning of the Reformation, dared to challenge medieval Catholic understanding that institutional mediation was a *sine qua non* to reach divine favor. And, subsequently, Protestantism taught that individuals could have a personal relationship with God

---

1 John Wesley, *Journals and Diaries I, 1735–38, Works*, 18:153. According to this volume's organizers (W. Reginald Ward and Richard P. Heitzenrater), this phrase—whose origins go back to Jerome (*Epistles,* number 125)—was adopted by Bernard of Clairvaux and Francis of Assisi. In the same direction, we must recall the name of Thomas à Kempis, whose work indelibly marked Wesley's biography. This medieval mystic also insists in the total renouncement of oneself in order to attain "freedom of heart" (see *The Imitation of Christ.* Book III, 37, 3 [Chicago: Moody Publishers, 2007], 249–51).

2 See Sermon 48, "Self-denial," *Works* (Jackson). When someone tries to disqualify the evangelical demand (Luke 9:23), alleging that "the mystic writers teach self-denial," Wesley reacts quickly: "No; the inspired writers! And God teaches it to every soul who is willing to hear his voice!" (§ III, 2).

and needed no intermediary. B. B. Warfield translates this change of focus this way: "The Reformation, inwardly considered, was just the ultimate triumph of Augustine's doctrine of grace over Augustine's doctrine of the church."[3] The end result of this process was the divorce between the doctrines of salvation and the church. While Roman Catholics in general reinforced the visibility and the role of the church in history, or, more strictly, its ecclesiastical hierarchy, Protestants tended to spiritualize the message of salvation, fully stripping it of its social content. With no dialogue or interaction, debate almost always ended with a choice between ecclesiocentrism[4] and individualism.

This impasse was projected in the interpretation of Wesleyan ecclesiology, and it was not long before the founders of Methodism were listed as partisans of one or another tendency.[5] On one hand, Wesley's Anglican

---

3 Alister E. McGrath, *Reformation Thought: An Introduction* (Oxford: Baker Book House, 1995), 188.

4 We employ here the word *ecclesiocentrism* to mean the understanding of the church by itself and for itself. In this understanding, as a divine institution, the church is identified to the kingdom of God with no distinctions whatsoever. It becomes an absolute value and is confused with salvation itself. To become part of ecclesiastical structures is seen as effectively participating in the work of redemption. Thus, excommunication entails immediate departure from God and, therefore, eternal damnation. To sum it up, the church is interpreted as an end in itself and not as a means of grace.

5 Despite significant exceptions, specific systematic studies about Wesley's thinking on the church are relatively recent. We must mention two doctoral theses: Seok Oh Gwang, *John Wesley's Ecclesiology: A Study in Its Sources and Developmen*t (Lanham, MD: The Scarecrow Press, Inc., 2007); and José Carlos de Souza, *Leiga, Ministerial e Ecumênica: A Igreja no Pensamento de John Wesley [Lay, Ministerial and Ecumenical: The Church in the Thought of John Wesley]* (São Bernardo do Campo: Editeo, 2009). The following paragraphs are based in the research and books that are part of the latter title. We must also refer to David Carter, *Love Bade Me Welcome: A British Methodist Perspective on the Church* (London: Epworth, 2002), 197, which offers an overview of United Kingdom Methodist ecclesiology, starting with John and Charles Wesley. Recently, some theologians from the Church of the Nazarene have published a collective work addressing fundamental aspects of the doctrine of the church in a Wesleyan perspective. See Diane Leclerc & Mark A. Maddix, eds., *Essential Church: A Wesleyan Ecclesiology* (Kansas City: Beacon Hill Press, 2014). These twenty articles aim at understanding the nature, functions, and constitution of the church.

heritage and repeated claims of loyalty to the Church of England all through his life were invoked to reinforce the "catholicizing" elements of his thought. John, and moreover Charles, never completely abandoned what has conventionally been called the High Church. Indeed, during his youth, consonant with the education he received from his family, John Wesley identified with the conservative piety of the "nonjurors"—a group so called due to their reluctance to take oaths to Queen Mary, daughter of James II, who was deposed in 1688, and her husband, William of Orange. Wesley's attachment to a hierarchical understanding of the church as a community of liturgy and devotion, based on the authority of the bishops through an unbroken succession since the time of the apostles, is evident during his formation at Oxford and his missionary experience in the British colony of Georgia. He certainly would not have hesitated to restrict the meaning of the famous axiom by Cyprian of Carthage—"*extra ecclesiam nulla salus*"[6]—to "Without formal adherence to the Church of England, there is no salvation." In practice this led Wesley to refuse the Eucharist to people whose baptism he judged as invalid, just because they had been baptized by "ministers" with no episcopal ordination—a zeal that not even many English theologians shared. Even though they acknowledge that this view was somewhat attenuated afterward, scholars that link Wesley to a Catholic conception of the church are quick to trace this identification with, for instance, his high sense of historical continuity; respect for sacred orders and the priestly ministry; value of patristic literature; accent on Christian unity; firm refusal to separate from the Church of England; and intense attachment to sacramental practice, especially the Lord's Supper.

On the other hand, however, are scholars who claim that Wesley was a fervent supporter of the evangelical cause. To these, the 1738 experience at Aldersgate was a real watershed.[7] Contact with the Moravians had served

6 Translated: "Outside the Church, there is no salvation."

7 The place and meaning of the warm-hearted experience of Wesley, as the Methodists call it, are at least polemical. The subject is surrounded by countless interpretations. See among others: Theodore W. Jennings, "John Wesley against Aldersgate," in *Quarterly Review: A Journal of Scholarly Reflection for Ministry* 8, no. 3 (Nashville: The United Methodist Publishing House and the United Methodist Board of Higher

to reconnect Wesley to his ancestors' Puritanism; and, by extension, to the precious legacy of the Reformation, especially to the experience of justification by grace and faith. This change of heart led to a total reorientation of his theology and practice. From then on Wesley would conceive his ecclesiology with an emphasis and focus on soteriology. There are those who even advocate a certain reprint of what had occurred in the sixteenth-century reform movement, the victory of the doctrine of grace over the doctrine of the church.

However, we must undo some serious interpretative misconceptions. It is certain that the peculiar emphasis on the path of salvation is an indispensable corrective to the overestimation of the church as a sacred institution, an historical concretion of the kingdom of God announced by Jesus. This does not imply at all, however, a mere suppression of ecclesiological interest. Wesley really did not sublimate his ecclesial concerns. He actually abandoned the static and formal understanding of the church that at first dominated his theology in favor of another ecclesiology, which may be more properly characterized as dynamic, functional, and organic. This ecclesiology—as well as his entire thinking—is both experimental and practical, deeply rooted in the simple life of the poor. To abandon the church's importance is to leave doors wide open to fostering pure individualism, here understood according to common sense, as the tendency or "attitude of those who reveal little or no solidarity and try to live exclusively for their own sake."[8] As Howard Snyder cautions:

> There is a strong tendency among Evangelicals to dissolve ecclesiology into the immediacy of personal Christian experience—a tendency, in the name of functionality, to make the question of

---

Education and Ministry, Fall 1988): 3–22; Randy L. Maddox, ed., *Aldersgate Reconsidered* (Nashville: Abingdon Press, 1990); and José Carlos de Souza, *"Aldersgate, uma tradição inventada? A experiência de John Wesley e nós hoje"* ["Aldersgate, an invented tradition? The experience of John Wesley and us today"], in *Experimentar Deus Hoje: A propósito dos 275 anos da experiência religiosa de John Wesley* (São Bernardo do Campo: Editeo, 2014), 55–72.

8 *Dicionário Eletrônico Houaiss da língua portuguesa* [Houaiss Electronic Portuguese Dictionary] (Rio de Janeiro: Objetiva, 2001).

> normative patterns of shared Christian life irrelevant. This tendency testifies not only to the individualism of much contemporary Christianity but also to a kind of sociological naïveté.[9]

Wesley does not fit this profile in any way.[10]

Salvation, which includes both justification and sanctification, is not the lonely trajectory of faithful individuals illuminated by the Word and the divine Spirit. Saving faith, because it is "faith which worketh by love," as one of his favorite biblical passages (Gal. 5:6 KJV) affirms, does not develop apart from life in community. Following Christ involves not only an ascetic stripping, renouncement, and self-denial, but chiefly an opening up to other persons—regardless of opinions and practices—for the mutual exercise of solidarity and the readiness to support one another's burdens.

What caught Wesley's attention regarding the Moravians was not only the preaching of God's forgiveness through faith. Rather, he first observed the communal lifestyle they cultivated, dividing themselves into small groups, through which men and women ministered to others through acts of mercy and charity as part of their responsibilities to the people of God. Bit by bit his mind assimilated a radical conception of the church that included laity, not only admitting them as observers, but actually creating practical ways to develop the universal priesthood of all believers. Not only this, but Wesley became increasingly aware of the potential of Nikolaus

---

9 Howard Snyder, "Spirit and Form in Wesley's Theology: A response to Keefer's 'John Wesley: Disciple of Early Christianity,'" in *Wesleyan Theological Journal* 19, no. 1 (1984): 35. Online version available at: http://wesley.nnu.edu/fileadmin/imported_site/wesleyjournal/1984-wtj-19-1.pdf, accessed November 25, 2010.

10 Despite many reductionist interpretations of Wesley's legacy, the general opinion of scholars studying his thought points to another direction, as Runyon observes: "One of the reasons Wesley is such an interesting figure is that he combines both an early stage of pietistic individualism and a vigorous protest against it." Theodore Runyon, *The New Creation: John Wesley's Theology Today* (Nashville: Abingdon Press, 1998), 103.

von Zinzendorf's model of "diaspora societies"[11] for the reformation of the Church of England, which became for him the absolute priority.[12]

Obviously, Wesley assimilated this influence critically, although not rejecting the path he had gone through. In particular, he criticized the Moravian tendency of depreciating ecclesiastical ordinances, especially sacramental practice. He also had difficulty accepting their tendency toward antinomianism,[13] because of their emphasis on the religion of the heart, which ended up weakening the Christian life's ethical dimensions and had disastrous consequences in terms of standing in solidary with neighbors, especially poor people. Unfortunately, those who emphasize the *evangelical character* of Wesleyan ecclesiology do not always recall that the reticence revealed by Wesley on the indicated aspects led him to split with the Moravian community. If the formal occasion for this rupture, which happened in 1740, was over the so-called "stillness controversy," the reasons were already somehow underlying his theology.

---

11 See Souza, *Leiga, Ministerial e Ecumênica* 47, 119–21, 208. Diaspora societies kept people united around common ideals and the same faith but without breaking with confessional loyalty and without imposing a rupture with the local congregation. See also Frederick A. Dreyer, *The Genesis of Methodism* (Bethlehem, PA: Lehigh University Press, 1999), 61ff: "In its largest sense, *diaspora* refers to Christians who are real believers. They may belong to any denomination, but as members of the *diaspora* they find their unity in the invisible church of Christ."

12 Wesley's interpretation of the role of the Methodist movement is well known, as follows: "*Q.3.* What may we reasonably believe to be God's design in raising up the Preachers called Methodists? *A.* Not to form any new sect; but to reform the nation, particularly the Church; and to spread scriptural holiness over the land" in *Minutes of Several Conversations between the Rev. Mr. John Wesley and others; from the year 1744 to the year 1789, The Works of the Rev. John Wesley* (London: Wesleyan-Methodist Book-Room, n.d., vol. 8, 299).

13 Extreme emphasis on the *sola fide* principle led to total disdain (anti = against) for the works of the law (from the Greek *nomós*). As with the apostle Paul (Rom. 3:21-31), Wesley did not accept legalism but also firmly rejected the antinomian understanding. See, for instance, the series of Wesley's sermons numbered 34, 35, and 36, respectively, "The Original, Nature, Property, and Use of the Law" and "The Law Established Through Faith," Discourses I and II.

Some scholars of Wesleyan thought suggest that Wesley, in his theological maturity, knew how to conjugate elements that normally appear dissociated in different branches of Christian tradition, notwithstanding their differences about what should come first. Aspects of various ecclesiological currents mentioned above appear combined in Wesley's reflections. Therefore, it would be foolish to connect him unilaterally to one or another ecclesiological tendency. Outler notes, in a comment to Wesley's seventy-fourth sermon ("Of the Church"), that, despite being written in the heat of 1784's controversy about the ordination for American Methodists, this is the first formal synthesis of his ecclesiology and that his conclusions can hardly be labeled Anglican, Lutheran, or Calvinist. It is actually "an unstable blend of Anglican and Anabaptist ecclesiologies; it is also one of Wesley's most daring syntheses."[14] Employing common expressions to Latin American theology, one can say that many aspects—the official and the sectarian, tradition and renewal, the formal and the spontaneous, order and charisma, institution and movement, and lastly, what is ecclesiastical and what is ecclesial—are integrated, giving birth to a surprising reconceptualization of the church, one that is hard to apprehend. After noting that the Methodist societies were catalysts of the movement of renewal and change, Paul Chilcote highlights their ability to integrate and hold together some elements, which usually were in opposition:

> They affirmed both the necessity of a personal, vital relationship with God, lived out in the intimacy of small groups, and the necessity and validity of the institutional church in its historical form. Their view of the community of faith combined the truths they found in both the institutional and the charismatic understanding of the church. Either was deficient without the other. An emphasis upon order and an appreciation for the past can become lifeless if not celebrated presently in the Spirit; the celebration of the Spirit as an animating force within the life of the church can become divisive and self-serving if not rooted in a timeless heritage of faith.

14 John Wesley, *Sermons III* in *Works*, 3:45–46.

A past-filled-with-gratitude and a present-filled-with-wonder as it looks to the future need to be held together.[15]

It is almost impossible to ignore the parallels between this description and the basic intuition of Leonardo Boff's ecclesiology, especially in his work *Church, Charism and Power*,[16] as the title itself suggests. From the experiences of the simple people of the faith communities, both Wesley and Boff seek to articulate characteristics that are often in opposition. But the similarities go well beyond mere theoretical affinity. Neither Boff nor Wesley show any intention of maintaining, by itself, a position of theological balance, a kind of middle road between two opposite poles. The actual life of communities of faith lies at the root of both theologians' concerns, notably the life of impoverished people who had to rely solely on divine grace and strength gleaned from their bonds of communion and solidarity. Just as with the Latin-American experience, Wesley was indeed at the forefront of a movement of intense ecclesial fermentation, whose vitality was the result of simple people refusing to be mere objects of pastoral assistance carried

15 Paul Wesley Chilcote, *Recapturing the Wesleys' Vision: An Introduction to the Faith of John and Charles Wesley* (Downers Grove, IL: InterVarsity Press, 2004), 62.

16 See Leonardo Boff, *Church: Charism and Power: Liberation Theology and the Institutional Church* (Eugene, OR: Wipf and Stock Publishers, 2012; 1st edition in Portuguese, 1981); *Ecclesiogenesis: The Base Communities Reinvent the Church* (Maryknoll, NY: Orbis Books, 1986; 1st edition in Portuguese, 1977); *E a Igreja se fez Povo. Eclesiogênese: A Igreja que nasce da fé do Povo* [*And the Church became People. Ecclesiogenesis: The Church that is born from the faith of the People*] (Petrópolis: Vozes, 1986). The significant parallels between Leonardo Boff's thought and evangelical theology have been highlighted by Rudolf von Sinner in "*Leonardo Boff—um católico protestante*" ["Leonardo Boff—a Protestant Catholic"], in *Estudos Teológicos* 46, no. 1 (São Leopoldo: Escola Superior de Teologia, 2006): 152–73. In the quoted author's opinion, Boff's understanding of the church "resonates very positively as Protestant theology, better still, evangelical—since it insists on the people of God as reference to the Church," and on its governance under the prism of service (156). This Lutheran theologian adds afterward: "Boff's ecclesiology is an ecclesiology 'from the bottom,' from the people—in Protestant terminology, of the universal priesthood of believers (see 1 Pet. 2:9), a participative ecclesiology rooted in faith and in the Gospel" (157). No doubt Wesley would endorse such understanding.

out by ordained ministers, in favor of constituting themselves into agents of transformation, both of the church and society. The church, so to speak, was reborn from the base, just as in the early days of Christianity when, day by day, people were incorporated into its ranks, which the ruling elites deeply disdained.

It is not an overstatement to say that Wesley developed an authentic daily-life ecclesiology, because ecclesial living comes before any ecclesiological statement. First, the Church is "the theater of divine wisdom" (*Explanatory Notes upon the New Testament*: Eph. 3:10) and a space where the grace of God is manifest in favor of all humanity, especially the "least of these." Only afterward does ecclesiology emerge; that is, reflection upon daily practices illuminated by Christian revelation. Indeed, Wesley did not execute a previously conceived program, nor did he actualize an ecclesiastical theory, elaborated according to the canons and methodological procedures derived from rigid orthodoxy. In accounts of the beginnings of Methodist practices, Wesley almost always accentuated the initiatives of the communities in facing ordinary problems or in the pursuit of agreed objectives, especially for the purpose of spreading holiness of heart and life. These communities of the faithful honed their structure as they sought to provide what was needed as they went about, dynamically and functionally, configuring the movement's identity.

Thus what Wesley designated as prudential means of grace took shape: aids developed by human creativity, based on scripture, reason, experience, church teaching, and the observation of the natural world, to meet the circumstantial demands of following Christ and the *missio Dei*.[17] These

---

17 Wesley never questioned the Bible's centrality. However, he did not dismiss from theological understanding the contributions offered by other references, thus composing what has been called the "Wesleyan Quadrilateral" (Albert C. Outler). Despite never employing this terminology nor systematically reflecting on the subject, this interpretation is coherent, moreover because it can be grounded on his writings. Brazilian Wesleyan studies have critiqued the fact that this interpretation has left aside the "wisdom of God in the Creation," according to the fortunate expression Wesley coined. This subject has been discussed in international events, such as the 11th Institute of The Oxford Institute of Methodist Theological Studies, August 2002 (see José Carlos de Souza, "Creation, New Creation and

included, among other things, organizing societies, class meetings, and bands (in all their different forms); participating in love feasts, vigils, and conferences; visiting sick and imprisoned people; structuring opportunities for benevolence and charity; giving monetary loans, having zeal for health, clinics, and care of children; and founding schools and other institutions designed to meet and foster all these modes of missionary action.

Active involvement in these ministries prevented people from becoming complacent in the religious societies organized by the first Methodists. Although not everyone preached at society meetings, everyone was entitled to speak, share difficulties and expectations, and, together, seek common answers, establish routines, deliberate on methods, and carry out roles that they would never have had the opportunity to hold in the majority of the Church of England's parishes at that time. Despite not having specific offices, no one was exempted from the responsibility of "carry[ing] each other's burdens" (Gal. 6:2 NIV). Therefore, far from being a solitary practice, Christian discipleship took shape in an historic form of ecclesial communion. This was especially evident when members fully and irrevocably committed themselves to their neighbors, particularly those who were at the margins of social and ecclesial life. Hence there is no doubt that the ecclesial communion was always open to the outside.

The dynamics and intensity of this commitment may be gauged by reading Wesley's *Journal*, where he describes how simple people—men, women, and children, young and old—embodied the gospel in ordinary life situations. He often showed how ordinary people, as so many even today, reflect the image of God in their dedication and self-giving to others,

---

Theological Method in Wesleyan Perspective," accessed August 18, 2017, https://oimts.files.wordpress.com/2013/04/2002-2-souza.pdf, and has found strong resonance among North American scholars. See, among others, Sarah H. Lancaster, "Current debates over Wesley's legacy among his progeny," in *The Cambridge Companion to John Wesley*, ed. Randy L. Maddox and Jason E. Vickers (Cambridge: Cambridge University Press, 2010), 314; Randy L. Maddox "*Luz para o 'caminho da salvação': John Wesley e a Bíblia*," in *Teologia Wesleyana, Latino-Americana e Global: Uma Homenagem a Rui de Souza Josgrilberg* (São Bernardo do Campo: Editeo, 2011), 83–85; Howard A. Snyder, *Wesley, a Bíblia e o Povo* (São Bernardo do Campo: Editeo, 2012), 18–19, 30–31.

thereby clearly imitating Christ. In the following account, he pays plain but meaningful homage to a recently deceased member of the movement:

> Sarah Peters, a lover of souls, a mother in Israel, went to rest. During a close observation of several years, I never saw her, upon the most trying occasions, in any degree ruffled, or discomposed, but she was always loving, always happy. It was her peculiar gift and her continual care, to seek and to save that which was lost; to support the weak; to comfort the feeble-minded, to bring back what had been turned out of the way. And in doing this, God endued her above her fellows, with the love that "believeth, hopeth, and endureth all things" (*Journal*, Nov. 13, 1748).[18]

This is a beautiful image of the spirit that gives life to the church as a community of God's people that, despite its failures, seeks to signal divine love for those who suffer—those who are lost, weak, or cast to the margins. The imitation of Christ, who emptied himself and made himself a gift for others, finds its place in communities that live in co-responsible discipleship and translate face-to-face encounters into sharing and solidarity. Self-denial becomes service that restores life and expresses itself through many gifts for mutual edification.

For Wesley, pastoral care was not a task of the clergy only but the natural fruit of the fellowship, mutual assistance, and encouragement that exemplified "faith which worketh by love" (Gal. 5:6 KJV) in the life of community. His perception was not at all exaggerated when one describes the Christian community as therapeutic. After all, being "Christ's mystical body," every member should be actively concerned with one another: "If one member suffers, all suffer together with it; if one member is honored, all rejoice together with it" (1 Cor. 12:26). In this context Wesley recalls the pagan commentary on Christians in the Roman Empire, as Tertullian put it in his *Apology* (§ 39, 7): "See how these Christians love one another."[19] The secret of the "force of the cure" becomes evident when someone, being overtaken in

---

18 John Wesley, *Journals and Diaries III, 1743-54* in *Works*, 20:252–53.

19 See Sermon 49, "The Cure of Evil-speaking"," § III, 5, in *Works*.

any sin, is corrected in the spirit of meekness by "every one who can" help (*Explanatory Notes upon the New Testament*: Gal. 6:1).

Lay involvement was essential to Wesley's understanding of the church. Although this aspect is not unique, it must not be underestimated. Diane Leclerc and Mark Maddix highlight three key elements in the Wesleys' church paradigm: worship (Word and sacraments), shared life, and missional engagement. Regarding the second, they comment:

> The church is a gathering where its people are intentionally present to each other. The church is a healing community, a place of deep acceptance, a place of compassion, kindness, humility, gentleness, patience, forbearance, forgiveness, and love [Col. 3:12-14].[20]

One would expect this way of life would appeal to other people. However, this was not always the case. The practices of early Methodists often stirred up unfavorable feelings. Wesley and his followers met with hostility, persecution, and countless accusations during almost the entirety of his ministry, often leading him to stand in defense of the societies associated with the movement.[21] Common criticisms were directed against lay preaching, itinerancy, and open-air worship, as well as the organization of the relatively autonomous societies. Wesley also weathered rebukes to the supposedly heretical content (Arminian, Pelagian) of his sermons and their enthusiastic, that is, fanatical, reception—at least in his opponents' judgment.

One of the most serious objections was that Methodists promoted schism, inciting division among Christians, leading them to withdraw from the church. Precisely because destroying fellowship touched a fundamental

---

20 Diane Leclerc and Mark A. Maddix, eds., *Essential Church: A Wesleyan Ecclesiology* (Kansas City: Beacon Hill Press, 2014), 18.

21 As in Christian origins, the Methodist movement was subjected to intense hostility and violence, especially in the 1740s. The causes of the strong opposition it faced were briefly analyzed by John Walsh in "Methodism and the Mob in the 18th Century," in *Popular Belief and Practice: Papers read at the 9th Summer Meeting and the 10th Winter Meeting of the Ecclesiastical History Society*, G. C. Cuming and Derek Baker, eds. (Cambridge: Cambridge University Press, 1972), 213–27. See also Henry D. Rack, *Reasonable Enthusiast: John Wesley and the Rise of Methodism* (London: Epworth Press, 2002), 270–81.

aspect of his ecclesiological understanding, Wesley answered firmly. In 1748, his friend and associate the Rev. Vincent Perronet, vicar of Shoreham, Kent, encouraged his response. Wesley simply asked: How is it possible to destroy something that never existed? Where is this found? In which parish? His questions targeted the center of the issue. The Methodist movement, by advocating mutual care and responsibility, drew those who had been far from Christian communion close and effectively integrated them into community life. It provided necessary support and tenderly cared for them, things not typically found in the majority of parish churches:

> Which of those true Christians had any such fellowship with these? Who watched over them in love? Who marked their growth in grace? Who advised and exhorted them from time to time? Who prayed with them and for them, as they had need? This, and this alone, is Christian fellowship.

Describing Methodist practices, Wesley turned his adversaries' reasoning on its head, categorically concluding: "We introduce Christian fellowship where it was utterly destroyed. And the fruits of it have been peace, joy, love, and zeal for every good word and work."[22] The presence of the Holy Spirit, evident through the experience of community and fellowship, was reminiscent of the first Christian communities (Acts 2:42-47; 4:32-35).

These arguments were unable, however, to undo the real motivation beneath the opposition Wesley's followers faced: social prejudice. Indeed, ever since its onset, the Methodist movement was stronger in attracting English society's impoverished *strata*, simple workers, men and women uprooted and marginalized by ongoing social processes that would eventually result in modern industrial civilization. Wesley not only rejected paternalism fed by politicians and priests but was willing to learn from the poor and, with them, developed means that ensured to them full participation. Many of those "irregularities," according to ecclesiastical rules in force, that were incorporated to the movement, were born by initiative or suggestion

22 "A Plain Account of the People Called Methodists" § I, 11 in *Works* (Jackson), 8:281–82.

of people who, having heard field preaching, joined the "people called Methodists"—one of Wesley's favorite expressions.

The proclamation of the universality of God's grace, free in all and free for all, helped undo the implicit elitism of the doctrine of predestination. Therefore, God could no longer be contained in the ordinary channels, since God's Spirit was acting through extraordinary means, challenging traditional preconceived schemes and even human rationality. However, there were criteria to identify God's action: personal and social transformation, the fruit of the Spirit, inner and outer holiness, the reformation of the church and of the nation; that is, the promotion of life, communion, justice, and solidarity. Thus, simple people gained their own voices and agency, no longer being mere listeners or passive objects for ecclesiastical leadership. To the contrary, they became social and ecclesial agents, able to discern, in communion with others, which direction they should take.

Self-proclaimed owners of both power and knowledge considered such pretense an intolerable affront. Can the people do theology? Can unordained men preach? And women? What are we to say about these uncultured masses willing to teach the gospel of Christ? The Calvinist Augustus Toplady had other reasons to oppose Wesley, beyond the issue of election and irresistible grace. He accused Wesley of defiling the holiness of ministry by encouraging wholly unqualified people to preach the divine Word. His recommendations to Wesley speak of sophisticated rhetoric and severe prejudice:

> Let his cobblers keep to their stalls. Let his tinkers mend their vessels. Let his barbers confine themselves to their blocks and basons. Let his bakers stand to their kneading-troughs. Let his blacksmiths blow more suitable coals than those of controversy.[23]

Although criticisms of this kind reverberated frequently in his writings, Wesley was unyielding. He was convinced that divine plans always follow their course, "from the least of them to the greatest" (Jer. 31:34; Heb. 8:11). For

23 In Howard A. Snyder, *The Radical Wesley and Patterns for Church Renewal* (Downers Grove, IL: InterVarsity Press, 1980), 64.

this reason, he recommended Methodist preachers seek the city's outskirts and not areas considered "noble." He himself followed literally this principle. Indeed, historical research on the social composition of the early Methodist movement shows that the majority of its adherents lived in pockets of poverty in urban centers and around coal mines. In one of the few occasions Wesley preached in an elegant neighborhood, he was pessimistic about his success and was quick to justify: "We begin at the wrong end. Religion must not go from the greatest to the least, or the power would appear to be of man" (*Journal*, May 21, 1764).[24] Thus, this proceeding is not about a simple missionary strategy but about obedience to God's design.

Consequently, from a Wesleyan perspective, ecclesiology must be first considered from the bottom and never from structures of power. The nature, purpose, constitution, functions, and mission of the church are adequately understood only at its base, where tensions are present and the grace of God in Christ manifests significantly and concretely, generating a new reality. David Hempton follows this line of thinking in his historical analysis of the origins of Methodism. He says that it "was a cultural revolution from below, not a political or ecclesiastical program imposed from above." It was not born from well-conceived plans by spiritual elites; it was built, step by step, by the simple people answering in faith the gospel's invitation. Hempton adds: "It was also a movement in search of a voice, which is why it was so noisy and so devoted to singing."[25] In practice, Wesley turned ecclesiology upside down. He made a radical inversion: questioning the priesthood's monopoly and valuing lay ministry; challenging dominant economic and political groups and organizing simple people; and putting

---

24 This and other passages reaffirming the same stance [*Explanatory Notes upon the New Testament*, Hebrews 8:11; Sermon 63, § 19] are meticulously analyzed in: Souza, *Leiga, Ministerial e Ecumênica*, 141–49. See also Joerg Rieger, *Grace under Pressure: Negotiating the Heart of the Methodist Tradition* (Nashville: General Board of Higher Education and Ministry, 2011), 20–23; Howard A. Snyder, *Wesley, a Bíblia e o Povo* (São Bernardo do Campo: Editeo, 2012), 17–18.

25 David Hempton, *Methodism: Empire of the Spirit* (New Haven and London: Yale University Press, 2005), 30–31. We cannot underestimate the importance Charles Wesley's hymns had in strengthening the ecclesial consciousness of the Methodist societies.

in check the ecclesiastical institution on behalf of missionary demands and community dynamics.

There is no way to know if Wesley was aware of his ecclesiology's revolutionary dimensions. Notwithstanding, it is correct to say that the Methodist movement's practices completely broke with the clerical and hierarchical understanding of that time. Seeing the church as a people, and not strictly in terms of its leadership, Wesley developed an ecclesiology that had a prominent place for laity (from the Greek *laikós*, "of the people," "popular"), revitalizing the New Testament understanding, which did not recognize distinctions based on holy orders.[26] The differences between ministries remained, but they were purely functional, establishing no pretention of superiority. Neither were they based on divine right. Before God, who alone is worthy of honor and worship, all are equal.

> But you are not to be called rabbi, for you have one teacher, and you are all students. And call no one your father on earth, for you have one Father—the one in heaven. Nor are you to be called instructors, for you have one instructor, the Messiah. (Matt. 23: 8-10)

Wesley is categorical in his comment on this passage. After describing the customs of the old alliance's rabbis, who required absolute loyalty, he observed: "Our Lord . . . , by forbidding us either to give or receive the title of rabbi, master, or father, forbids us either to receive any such reverence, or to pay any such to any but God" (*Explanatory Notes upon the New Testament,*

---

26 See Alexandre Faivre, *Os Leigos nas Origens da Igreja* (Petrópolis: Vozes, 1992); English version: *The Emergence of the Laity in the Early Church* (Mahwah, NJ: Paulist Press, 1990). After examining the meaning of the word *kleros* in the New Testament, especially in the Pauline *corpus* and in 1 Peter, the author maintains that such terminology is "applied to the entirety of the faithful, and not just reserved for ministers. . . . The priestly function, true priesthood, belongs to Christ that makes all Christians its participants. . . . The New Testament does not know laity, but a people, a holy people, a chosen people, a people set apart, a *kleros* that in its entirety exerts royal priesthood that calls each of its members to offer God true worship in spirit. It is useless to search the New Testament writings for a theology of laity: we find neither lay people nor priests in the personal sense we nowadays understand it" (p. 21 in Portuguese version).

Matt. 23:8-10). In the kingdom of God, performing a ministry is to assume the condition of a servant (Matt. 20:27), that is, to strip oneself of all pretenses and present oneself "naked to follow the naked Christ."

Thus, we return to the starting point, not, however, in the context of the personal search for salvation, but in the interrelationships of community life that are deeply connected to life and mission of the church. Here the ties between this "self-stripping" and the exercise of solidarity become visible. These ties are immanently present in the daily lives of the religious societies founded by Wesley and his followers. This is why it is a bit surprising that the expression *solidarity* never appears in his writings. The reason for such absence is simple. This is because the word *solidarity* first appeared in French around 1840 (well after Wesley), tied to juridical and philosophical discussions. But soon it was taken by those involved in social struggles—particularly those bound to the Socialist Flags. The basic idea is that there is a mutuality that binds people and social groups *in solidum*, solidly, in a way that the whole is contained in a part and the part is contained in the whole. We cannot understand our individual or social group destiny as separate from others. Solidarity presupposes, mainly: mutual commitment, empathy, respect for diversity, sharing, reciprocity, and communion[27]—realities we see in the lives of early Methodists.

For people to act in solidarity, they must recognize that, despite differences, all are important and share the same dignity. Solidarity presupposes a relationship among equals. There can be no solidarity within a community of hierarchies, of inequality, divided between those who teach and those who learn, among those who possess certain qualifications—wealth, power, wisdom, piety, and so forth—and those who are completely devoid

27 In the *Dicionário Eletrônico Houaiss da Língua Portuguesa* [*Houaiss Electronic Portuguese Dictionary*] (Rio de Janeiro: Objetiva, 2001), nine distinct meanings for the word *solidarity* are listed, among which we highlight: "commitment through which people obligate themselves to one another and each person to all others; a bond or mutual tie between two or many things and persons that depend on one another; feeling of sympathy, tenderness or piety for the poor, the unprotected, those suffering, those wronged, etc.; . . . mutuality of interests and duties; identity of feelings, of ideas, of doctrines . . ."

of them. When there is asymmetry, only paternalism can exist—charity at its worst—a kind of unidirectional movement by those who feel superior toward those who are considered inferior: a movement from the top to the bottom. Never solidarity!

Final Considerations

Wesleyan ecclesiology has moved in the opposite direction of paternalism and authoritarianism. In the origins of the Methodist movement, the hierarchical principle did not prevail, but a fundamental egalitarianism, born from below, from the base. Each member of the community was valued and contributed to the common good. No voice was ignored. Differences of opinion were not obstacles to communion; instead they were incorporated in the whole. Each one's effort was recognized as both an expression of human diversity and a result of the action of the Spirit of God. If God employs the means God pleases, no person should judge oneself superior to others. Lay people, both man and woman, are responsible one to another, and everybody to the edification of the community. At a time when the right to life was denied to the poor, whose hope seemed to be solely the benevolence of the wealthy classes, the Methodists dared to encourage the autonomy, interdependence, organization, mutual care, participation, and leadership of plain people not only in the church but also in the society. They were no longer victims of an unjust and inhuman system, but agents of social as well as ecclesial change. Hence the outcome could be nothing other than solidarity.

Seen from this perspective, imitation of Christ is not an exclusive challenge for individual believers but a call for the whole community. The phrase "naked to follow the naked Christ" is thus an imperative to the church itself. We should expect that the church, like Christ, not only conceal but truly renounce any glory or influence it may enjoy or exert (See *Explanatory Notes upon the New Testament,* Phil. 2:7). This renunciation implies the revision of what is a priority for the mission of the church: institutional strengthening or service of the needy populations; increase of clerical authority or implementation of popular participation in ecclesial life; influence in the circles of power or struggle for human rights and social justice; prestige among respectable citizens or fidelity to the gospel message; numerical growth of their membership or commitment to the kingdom of God, and so on. These are not simple alternatives. But one wonders how far churches can hide behind structures of power that deny in practice the gospel. Churches need to present themselves naked, without false security, to serve the people, not themselves. Anyway, when institutional survival seems to be the great motive moving all ecclesiastical structures, it may sound absurd to affirm that the church must seek self-emptying, or that *kenosis* is the mark of ecclesial living with solidarity. However, perhaps this is the only way the church can be recognized as the body of Christ and a signal of hope to the world.

7

New Birth and Regeneration

Gratitude for and Commitment to God's Gift of Grace and the Willingness to Fight for Its Defense

Helmut Renders

Introduction

Why talk about "new birth" or about "regeneration"? It is because they allow us to continue the search for what it means to be human beings in continuous transformation, which some conclude was one of the twentieth century's tragic obsessions.[1] Others affirm that this search must continue, because this is pertinent to the survival of our species and our world,[2] despite the frantic twenty-first-century bet on innovation as a solution to

1 Nicola Lepp, Martin Roth, and Klaus Vogel, eds., *Der neue Mensch: Obsessionen des 20 Jahrhunderts* (Katalog zur Ausstellung im Deutschen Hygiene-Museum Dresden, 22.04.-08.08.1999 [*The New Human Being: Obsessions of the 20th Century* (Dresden: Hygiene-Museum Dresden, 1999)]).

2 "The Achilles' Heel of any program for sustainability is individual and institutional willingness or unwillingness of embracing a simpler lifestyle which is less aggressive and less exploitative to one's neighbor, to one's ecosystem and to future generations. In order to overcome possible standoffs, we need to form human being's character better, whose knowledge, attitude and vision may forge a *homo ecologicus*, or, better still, a *homo sustentabilis*." M. Silva, "*Homo sustentabilis*" in "*Folha de São Paulo*" (10/20/2008): n.p.

our world's problems, especially competition and consumption. For Christianity, a Wesleyan approach to new birth and regeneration is important, especially in Latin America.

In Pentecostal theology we see the ideas of new birth and regeneration played out in the understanding of baptism in the Holy Spirit as a specific way of talking about anthropogenesis—the regeneration of the human being. It is not by chance that these appear in Catholic theology as a search for ecclesiogenesis—a concept liberation theology uses.[3] In Wesleyan theology the hope for anthropogenesis and ecclesiogenesis is also articulated through the concept of reformation (of the church) and transformation (of the human being), amplified also by the conviction for the need to reform the nation, or as Wesley combined them: "to reform the nation, particularly the church, and to spread holiness over the country."[4] So, talking about new birth and regeneration as components of Wesleyan theology, as a way of answering the yearnings of the world we live in and in dialogue with other answers to these yearnings, might be surprisingly up to date.

Another aspect found in John Wesley's theology that favors this approach to new birth and regeneration was evident in the lectures of 2014's Wesleyan Week.[5] Wesley addressed new birth and regeneration not through speculation but by examining its effects by asking: What are the fruits of a human being's new birth and regeneration under God's grace-filled influence? What privileges and duties do human beings have regarding their individual lives, the lives of others, and the life of the entire creation? To whom is one reborn? What for? Wesleyan theology rarely discusses theology in and of itself. It does so only in relation to the world as a whole, to the world people live in, and to the people themselves. We might call this a soteriological emphasis. Thus, it is not by chance that all speakers of

---

3 Leonardo Boff, "*Eclesiogênese: As comunidades eclesiais de base re-inventam a Igreja,*" SEDOC IX (1976), 393–438; Leonardo Boff, ed., *Eclesiogênese: As Comunidades Eclesiais de Base Reinventam a Igreja* (Petrópolis: Vozes, 1977).

4 John Wesley, *Works* (Jackson), 8:299.

5 Wesleyan Week is an annual conference of the Theological School of the Methodist Church in Brazil, dedicated to themes concerning Methodist doctrine, history, or mission.

2014's Wesleyan Week dealt with soteriology, as exemplified by the lectures of Joerg Rieger and José Carlos de Souza, also contained in this publication.

In this essay, we will follow this direction and propose a discussion of the metaphors of rebirth and regeneration from a soteriological perspective. In Wesleyan theology this involves, generally, a perspective regarding salvation in a theological sense, encompassing a discourse that starts with the grace of God—giving human responsibility in receiving this divine action primacy over and above all human actions. The relation between human responsibility and the importance of the human ability to respond to the divine gift of grace, also described as divine-human synergy in the processes of salvation, was addressed by this 2014's Wesleyan Week keynote speaker Joerg Rieger in discussing grace as liberating—a transforming grace that liberates both "from" and "for." This means that grace is a power to engage new precepts and viewpoints, thanks to a new horizon: saved by grace, liberated to discover and appropriate all dimensions of Christian life, and liberated to reform the nation, including the church.

We will review the metaphors of rebirth and regeneration from this perspective to ensure, on the one hand, knowledge and understanding of traditional aspects and, on the other hand, to address more contemporary challenges. In the first section, "Being Born Again and the Regeneration of the Human Being: Gratitude for Life as a Divine Gift," we review the biblical witness found in the New Testament to explore afterward the original meaning of the metaphors, as they refer to a specific moment in the human life cycle. We will link the discussion about rebirth and regeneration as they have been variously understood, from the Middle Ages to modern times, as sacramental transmission or personal perception. In the second section, "Being Born Again, Regeneration and New Creation: Commitment to Life as Divine Gift and Natality," we first dialogue with biblical scholar Beth M. Stovell regarding her observation of the parallel use of the metaphors of "God-that-gives-life" and the "Warrior-God."[6] Then we turn to Hannah Arendt's concept of "natality" as it relates to the metaphors of "rebirth" and

6 Beth M. Stovell, "The birthing Spirit, the childbearing God: metaphors of motherhood and their place in Christian discipleship," in *Priscilla Papers* 26, no. 4 (Oct/Dec 2012): 16–21.

"regeneration."[7] Thus, we enter a dialogue about these long-standing issues methodologically. Throughout, we will also establish dialogue with John Wesley's pastoral praxis and theological reflection. I am confident that the argument I will present is consistent with Wesley's theological intuitions about the events and processes that he describes regarding new birth and regeneration. In addition, this essay also offers a basis for engaging contemporary struggles for the humanization of human beings and the creation of a sustainable lifestyle.

Being Born Again and the Regeneration of the Human Being: Gratitude for Life as a Divine Gift

In the history of Christianity, the subject of new birth appears with distinct tones at different times. Historically for some, the ties between rebirth and infant baptism are so powerful that the mere practice of baptism became an act of transmitting grace irresistibly, thereby ensuring salvation permanently. To others, the relationship between rebirth and baptism is about the articulation of provenance or prevenient grace that prompts our gratitude to God for our human existence, and also the need for confirmation that baptism is effectual for salvation. For a third group, baptism is merely a human rite and witness, an expression of obedience to a divine commandment, a public act that fulfills and follows rebirth as an experience. In infant baptism, the metaphor of rebirth takes its most literal form.

In late modernity, however, we no longer start with a sacramental logic, but with the question: "Are you born again?"[8] This question presents a very specific idea about the metaphor of new birth, in the sense of religious experience as a kind of knowledge or a religious assurance of belonging to God. Regarding the cycle of life, one can understand that this experience can be tied with the passage from adolescence to adult life, characterized by a growing self-consciousness and increased religious autonomy,

---

7 Hannah Arendt, *Rhetorical Exploration of Rebirth Language in 1 Peter* (doctoral dissertation, University of Toronto Centre for the Study of Religion, 2011).

8 Admittedly, each age has its own questions. Nowadays, for instance, one can hear, "Have you got the vision?"

as well as the publicly registered right (religious maturity) and the ability to make religious decisions. This understanding conveys the modern conception of human beings, whose dignity is largely expressed by their individual choices and decisions. This interpretation of new birth represents continuity and a shift of the original meaning of the metaphor: first, it signals a radical change in the process of passing from one existential state to another (from non-perception to the conviction of personal belonging to God); second, the original idea that places birth at the beginning of the cycle of human life is definitely abandoned.

Interestingly, we find this tension in the works of John Wesley. As Karen Westerfield Tucker observes:

> His sermons and other writings that address baptism and the "new birth," when taken together, articulate historic Anglican teachings as well as an evangelical concern for a subjective experience of faith, resulting in an apparent tension. Wesley agreed with his Church that infants receiving the sacrament of baptism were at the same time born again. . . . Yet Wesley observed that some persons who claimed the new birth of their infant baptism had lost the "principle of grace" because of unrepentant sinful acts. In Wesley's mind, these persons needed to be "born again" a second time by a conscious experience of saving grace in order to receive the "circumcision of the heart." Thus, two spiritual births were necessary for most persons—a sacramental and objective one via ritual baptism and an experiential and subjective one by a "heart-warming" encounter with Christ through the power of the Holy Spirit. Although these two new births can be connected—the second birth may be viewed as a recovery of the grace received in the first—Wesley never specifically qualifies their relationship.[9]

Tucker comments that, despite Methodism not abandoning for a long time the idea of a first regeneration being a baptismal regeneration, the

9 Karen B. Westerfield Tucker, "Sacraments and Life-circle Rituals," in *The Cambridge Companion to American Methodism*, ed. Jason E. Vickers (Cambridge: Cambridge University Press, 2013), 141.

language for a sacramental regeneration vanished from the rituals of the Methodist Episcopal Church in the first three decades of the twentieth century: first from the rites of infant baptism; afterward from the rites of adult baptism.[10] However, as early as the first half of the eithteenth century, the idea of dedication of children to God is introduced, not, at first, as an alternative. This leads the Church of the Nazarene to include, in 1936, a ritual of dedication next to baptism,[11] followed by The United Methodist Church in 1968,[12] and by the Free Methodist Church in 1986.[13] According to Gayle Felton, this tendency began in the 1950s: "By the 1950s, infant baptism was understood largely as a ceremony of dedication focused on pledges of parental responsibility."[14]

Regarding southern Methodism, Brooks Holifield identified the same double perception already found in Wesley[15]—albeit with a tendency of ignoring sacramental tradition, in the wake of "revivalist enthusiasm" following their split from the Methodist Episcopal Church. Around the second half of the nineteenth century, the rite of infant baptism became distinct from Baptist (sign) and Anglican (a purely sacramental rebirth)[16] theologies. The southern theologian Summers, for example, referred to it as a "saving ordinance."[17] Thomas Osmond Summers[18] (1812–1882), along with John

10 Ibid., 142.

11 Ibid., 143.

12 Ibid., 145.

13 Ibid., 144.

14 Gayle Carlton Felton, "Baptism," in *Historical Dictionary of Methodism*, 3rd ed., eds. Charles Yrigoyen Jr. and Susan E. Warrick (Lanham: Scarecrow Press, 2013), 54. See also the absence of the subject of rebirth in William J. Abraham and David F. Watson, eds., "What is Baptism? A: Baptism is a holy covenant with God by which we are brought into God's household and initiated into the life of the church," in *Key United Methodist Beliefs* (Nashville: United Methodist Publishing House, 2013).

15 E. Brooks Holifield, *The Gentlemen Theologians: American Theology in Southern Theology in Southern Culture, 1795–1860*, 2nd ed. (Durham: Duke University Press, 2007), 165.

16 Ibid., 166.

17 Ibid., 167.

18 Thomas Osmond Summers, *Systematic Theology: A Complete Body of Wesleyan Arminian Divinity, Consisting of Lectures on the Twenty-Five Articles of Religion*

Dick[19] (1764–1833), a Scottish theologian of the Reformed Church, and William Burt Pope[20] (1822–1903), a northern theologian, were references for the theologian Eduardo E. Joiner,[21] who wrote the first Methodist dogmatic in Brazil.[22] We can find each viewpoint reflected in the official documents of the Methodist Church of Brazil throughout the twentieth century. In the 1934 *Cânones* (*Book of Discipline*), the first edition under fully Brazilian redaction, we read: "Article 326—Baptism is one of the two sacraments ordained by Jesus Christ and, as such, is not only a Christian's initiation into the church but also a symbol of regeneration."[23]

In the 1965 edition, we read:

> Article 290—Sacraments are means of grace instituted by our Lord Jesus Christ, visible signs of the Holy Spirit's invisible grace in the life of believers. . . . Article 292—Baptism is the visible sign of the grace of our Lord Jesus Christ, through which we become participants in the communion of the Holy Spirit and heirs to eternal life.[24]

The absence of the word *regeneration* in this text echoes the discussions in The United Methodist Church; however, it preserves the notion of a performative

---

(Nashville: Publishing House of the M.E. Church, South, 1888).

19 John Dick, *Lectures on Theology* (Oxford: David Christy, 1836).

20 William Burt Pope, *A Compendium of Christian Theology: Being Analytical Outlines of a Course of Theological Study, Biblical, Dogmatic, Historical*, 3 volumes (Cleveland, OH: Thomas & Mattill, 1881).

21 Eduardo E. Joiner, *Theologia Christã: Sendo uma Apresentação e Defesa da Fé Christã Como é Ensinada Pelos Methodistas*, 2nd ed., vol. 2 (Rio de Janeiro: Casa Publicadora Methodista, 1900). In the chapter on "Regeneration" (77–95), Joiner follows the northern interpretation! Dialoguing with Catholic, Anglican, and Calvinist theology, he rejects any form of sacramental regeneration, as well as the passivity of the soul in the process of regeneration.

22 Around this time they also published another book in translation: Edmund Tilly, *Doutrinas Christãs: Com Introdução Pelo Rev. Dr. John M. Kyle* (Rio de Janeiro: Casa Publicadora Methodista, 1898).

23 *Igreja Metodista, Cânones da Igreja Metodista do Brasil* (São Paulo: Imprensa Metodista, 1934), 142.

24 *Cânones da Igreja Metodista do Brasil* (1965), 155–56.

act able to turn someone into something else. The ritual appearing in 1990 describes "the biblical meaning of baptism as a consecration of the child to God, and his/her introduction into the community of faith."[25] Any sacramental or performative understanding of baptism is gone. Here, only the idea of dedication prevails. This affirmation is not present in 2001's *Ritual* (*Book of Worship*),[26] and rightly so, because it contradicts the second part of Article 17, which, with the words "not only . . . but also," marks a mediating position: "Article 17: Baptism is not only a sign of profession of faith and a distinguishing mark that differentiates Christians from the unbaptized, but also a sign of regeneration, or new birth. Infant baptism must be preserved in the Church."[27] "Not only / but also" is an attempt to maintain this double understanding of new birth, the fundamental importance of the means of grace and of human responsibility, which results from grace, with no regard to human conscious action or free choice.[28]

On the following page a table appears of New Testament texts in what is considered chronological order. Here are six books that refer to the group of related terms: "rebirth," being "born again," being "born of" in Matthew, Titus, 1 Peter, 1 John, the Gospel of John, and James.

Despite employing the same root (James excluded)—the Greek γεν—the translation into Portuguese refers to being "born" only in the Johannine epistles and James. The four other texts employ "regenerate" or "regeneration."[29] Not only that, but this root is combined with different prefixes— παλιν and ανα—or different adverbs and conjunctions, such as ανωθεν and εκ. These differences represent distinct aspects: εκ articulates the origins or cause of new birth or regeneration, whereas παλιν and ανα stress the radically new character of new birth or regeneration. The fact

25 *Igreja Metodista, Ritual da Igreja Metodista* (São Paulo: Imprensa Metodista, 1990), 7.

26 *Ritual da Igreja Metodista* (2001); likewise in its 2005 2nd edition.

27 *Igreja Metodista, Cânones 2002* (São Paulo: Editora Cedro, 2007), 37.

28 Notice how this dialectic is relevant in Christology. For instance, regarding John 3:16 and 10:17-18: "The reason my Father loves me is that I lay down my life—only to take it up again. No one takes it from me, but I lay it down of my own accord. I have authority to lay it down and authority to take it up again."

29 Other translations (e.g., Martin Luther's) favor the concept of "new birth."

Year	Source	English	Greek
80–90 AD	Matthew 19:28	"at the renewal[a] of all things, when the Son of Man sits on his glorious throne, you who have followed me"	παλιγγενεσία
80–90 AD	Titus 3:5	"He saved us through the washing of rebirth[b] and renewal by the Holy Spirit"	παλιγγενεσία
90 AD	1 Peter 1:3	"he has given us new birth[c] into a living hope"	ἀναγεννῶ
90 AD	1 Peter 1:23	"For you have been born again,[d] not of perishable seed, but of imperishable, through the living and enduring word of God"	ἀναγεννῶ
95 AD	1 John 2:29 1 John 5:1	"has been born of him" "is born of God"[e]	γεννῶ ἐκ
95 AD	1 John 3:9 1 John 4:7 1 John 5:4 1 John 5:18	"born of God"	γεννῶ ἐκ
100–110 AD	John 3:3 John 3:7	"Born again"	γεννῶ ἄνωθεν
100–110 AD	John 3:6 John 3:8	"Spirit gives birth"[f] "Born of the Spirit"	γεννῶ ἐκ
100 AD	James 1:18	"He chose to give us birth through the word of truth, that we might be a kind of first fruits of all he created"	ἀπεκύησεν

a The Portuguese reading is "regeneration" (Translator's Note).

b The Portuguese reading is "regeneration" (Translator's Note).

c The Portuguese reading is "generated us again" (Translator's Note).

d The Portuguese reading is "regeneration" (Translator's Note).

e The Portuguese reading says "is born of Him" (Translator's Note).

f The Portuguese reading is "What is born of the flesh is flesh, what is born of the Spirit is Spirit" (Translator's Note).

that the same word is used only once by two different authors further complicates interpretation of new birth or regeneration as already established theological concepts, with a diffusion beyond local usage (what might be the case only of Matthew and Titus). In other words, from 80 to 100 AD, fixed terminology for this concept had not yet developed. Instead, we can see the evidence of local linguistic customs, and, eventually, local religious practices in the use of a metaphor, which cannot be reduced to a single meaning. Looking at the whole, we can identify four distinct aspects:

- The description of the bond between new birth/regeneration and baptism;
- The affirmation that new birth/regeneration strictly and only originates in God;
- The understanding of new birth/regeneration as liberation or empowerment for a new life;
- The establishment, through new birth/regeneration, of a continuous relationship between God and the person that is born again/ regenerated.

However, we have no one meaning that runs throughout all texts. Regarding the identification of new birth/regeneration with the rite of baptism, we can surely say that Titus refers to it, even though other biblical authors do not use it. In the case of 1 Peter, this connection is, at the very least, possible.[30] However, Matthew's eschatological understanding doesn't focus on this connection and, in the case of John and James, the relation to baptism is unassured, albeit not impossible. James, Titus, 1 Peter, 1 John, and the Gospel of John stress especially the divine origin of new birth/regeneration as an action either by the Father (1 Peter 1:3, 23; James 1:18; 1 John 2:29; 3:9; 4:7; 5:1, 4; 5:18), or by the Spirit (John 3, 4 and 6), or by the Son (Titus 3:5). First Peter 1:23 ("imperishable", "incorruptible") and James 1:18 ("first fruits of

30 See Keir E. Hammer, *Disambiguating Rebirth* (2012), 216: "While both texts use rebirth language to provide their readers with a social or community identity and neither connects that language to the Christian rite of baptism, 1 Peter does not contrast this identity with other communities; instead, it incorporates other Christian communities within this familial structure."

all he created" [NIV]) both refer to the effects of baptism, while 1 Peter 1:23 mentions also the creation of a lasting bond between father and son ("living and enduring"). To summarize: any reduction to a single interpretation masks a wealth of meanings related to the metaphors of new birth/regeneration. However, one aspect seems central in all these texts: the affirmation of gratitude for a life of faith as a divine gift.

Let us now look at the metaphor of rebirth/new birth in and of itself.[31] Birth is neither the beginning, nor the end, nor the highest expression of human life with regard to the development of its fullest potential. Newborns are potential, full human beings, whose task from birth is to assume this potentiality and interact with it, become aware of their new belonging, and, in so doing, find out who they are. A growing notion of limitation, the ability to err and succeed, and the need to create meaning from life are part of the maturation process. Based on this understanding of birth within the cycle of life, we can notice certain shifts of meaning in the biblical use of the metaphor of "new birth."

A first shift occurs when we conflate *potential* with *current*. Here I might substitute *potential* for *current*, in the sense that new birth can take place only when persons are able to know what they are experiencing, and to understand the experience as corresponding with conscious acceptance. This interpretation, however, drifts away from the original meaning, because it confuses new birth with maturity in the sense of a more advanced moment in life.

A second shift happens when we separate *potential* from *current*. In this case, we talk about new birth as a *potential* moment, as if it were the pinnacle of what may be achieved in life, disregarding its *actualization* as an important part of human development in relation to its development

31 According to Cobb, Wesley also employed the analogy between natural and spiritual birth: "Before their physical birth human beings have sense organs, but they do not see or hear. At birth, instantaneously, or in a very brief time, their senses begin to function." Besides, Cobb also relates "new birth" to "prevenient grace," which allows for the inclusion of baptismal regeneration, but goes beyond it. See John B. Cobb Jr., *Grace and Responsibility: A Wesleyan Theology for Today* (Nashville: Abingdon Press, 1995), 97–99.

in religious terms. What sounds absurd when we think about the cycle of human life ends up occurring with regard to the cycle of religious life. Discarding the metaphor from its origins may cause the loss of important aspects of its meanings, even to the point of making them partially incomprehensible. Hence, theocentric or anthropocentric models are both unable to relate some specific moments of faith to the cycle of religious life.

To summarize: the reading of "new birth" as a metaphor, starting with the experience of human life, opens up a new way to relate the moment of new birth to the performative representation of the unconditional and universal grace of God conveyed by infant baptism. It is being born of God, of Christ, and of the Spirit that turns the new human being into a new creation, a participant of the kingdom, and an heir to eternal life—future and anticipated. Birth marks the beginning of a journey. It does not mark a full or complete relationship, in either the biological or spiritual cycle of human life. However, processes of appropriation of the divine reality are also needed during this course. From our perspective, however, this is not just a matter of overcoming sin or the alienation that marks human existence as a whole. The experience and consciousness of living under grace are no guarantee to fully overcoming the human separation from God. Rebirth is never immediate. For us, the experience of rebirth as self-awareness and confronting one's own sin deals with the question of human dignity. Dignity is constituted by being able to recognize oneself in the self's real condition and limitation, and also to acknowledge the transforming power of universal and unconditional divine grace—a divine gift.

Being Born Again, Regeneration, and New Creation: Commitment to Life as Divine Gift and Natality

This section starts by considering that Matthew 19:28 implies that regeneration, in its fullest sense, involves all creation. This is articulated in Wesleyan theology through its emphasis on the new creation[32] as part of "a living hope" (1 Pet. 1:3), which also involves the church because together we

32 See Theodore Runyon, *The New Creation: John Wesley's Theology Today* (Nashville: Abingdon Press, 1998).

are "first fruits of all his creatures" (James 1:18). This line of thought is clear in John Wesley's writing. He translates 2 Corinthians 5:17 as: "Therefore, if anyone be in Christ, there is a new creation,"[33] not a "new creature." Wesley thus describes human relationship to Christ as being inscribed in this new creation as a participant that benefits, acts, and curates. I have written about certain aspects of this new life, as described in Ephesians 2:15 and 4:24,[34] as they relate to John Wesley's theology and Brazilian Methodism.

Now, we turn to a discussion of Beth M. Stovell's work regarding "rebirth" as an action by a "childbearing God." While Stovell interprets rebirth in the larger context of metaphors for "mother,"[35] we are particularly interested in her interpretation of Isaiah 42:13-14 and the images of the childbearing God and the warrior God:

> Applying these overlapping metaphorical entailments of "warrior" and "childbirth" to God provides a unique perspective on God's power and intensity within Isaiah 42. . . . Much work has been done on the divine-warrior motif in the OT, but especially important for our study is how the divine warrior's picture of triumphant champion over Israel's enemies provides the impetus for a change in the childbirth metaphor. The childbirth metaphor, often associated with fear and possible defeat or death, is "turned on its head to describe YHWH's power."[36]

---

33 John Wesley, *Explanatory Notes upon the New Testament* (London: [s.e.], 1754), 457: 2 Cor. 5:17: "Therefore, if anyone be in Christ, there is a new creation."

34 Helmut Renders, "O uso das expressões duplas δικαιοσύνη (dikaiosúne) e σιότης (hosiótes) como δικαιοσύνη e εσεβέια (eusebeia) no Novo Testamento: base para uma presença pública da Igreja?" in Horizonte, Belo Horizonte, MG 11, no. 31 (jul./sept. 2013): 1042–53.

35 Beth M. Stovell, "The birthing Spirit, the childbearing God . . . " (2012), 16: "Within the New Testament (NT), childbearing and mothering metaphors serve an important role in redescribing the spiritual rebirth (Gal 4:29; John 3:3-8), describing the experience of Jesus' death and resurrection for the disciples (Matt 24:8; Mark 13:8; John 16:21); describing Jesus Christ (1 Pet 1:3, 23; 1 John 2:20; James 1:18), and Paul describing his relationship to the Thessalonian church (1 Thess 2:7)."

36 Ibid., 17.

According to Stovell, this proximity leads to a rereading—especially—of passages from the Gospel of John:

> Understanding the resonances in John 16 of both Isaiah 42 and John 3 suggests that a correction is necessary in our general conception of the birth metaphor in John 3. Many commentaries speak of the childbirth in John 3 as simple and painless because it is spiritual rather than physical, as though a spiritual stork dropped the child off in a nice, neat package. . . . Jesus' clarification that this birth is spiritual and not physical does not necessarily remove the metaphorical implications of possible pain and/or crisis. As the metaphor theories of George Lakoff and Mark Johnson suggest, our understanding of metaphor often moves from an original physical referent to its abstraction in metaphor. . . . Childbirth is a combination of expectancy and uncertainty. In many ways, birth, like the wind and the Holy Spirit, would be seen as a mystery in the ancient world. . . . This means that we need to consider pain and struggle as part of the Christian journey. The journey of second birth and of spiritual regeneration is not painless or without crisis; rather, we journey through the difficulties entailed in this new birth, because we know the hope and joy that exists here as well.[37]

This interpretation indicates many clues worth exploring. However, any transposition of attributes and experiences by a divine subject—the childbearing God—to a human being—a childbearing woman—requires caution. The metaphor in Isaiah and John is primarily about God. However, Stovell makes it clear that this analogy is fully articulated precisely by the metaphors of new birth and regeneration: "In this way, we will be like Christ in his journey from death to resurrection."[38] This discussion may be new to us. However, her ideas find echoes as early as the eighteenth century, with John Wesley, who spoke about the need to love God and humanity and the need to count with and assume persecution for the gospel. Wesley's

---

37 Ibid., 19.

38 Ibid.

sermon on Matthew 5:13-16, "You are the salt of the world! You are the light of the world!" mentions *persecution* twenty-six times:

> I shall endeavour to show, First, that Christianity is essentially a social religion; and that to turn it into a solitary one is to destroy it. . . . Not that we can in any wise condemn the intermixing solitude or retirement with society. . . . Yet such retirement must not swallow up all our time; this would be to destroy, not advance, true religion. . . . Another necessary branch of true Christianity is peacemaking, or doing of good. . . . And your patient continuance in well-doing . . . your calm, humble joy in the midst of persecution, your unwearied labour to overcome evil with good, will make you still more visible and conspicuous than ye were before.[39]

We find other references regarding *persecution* in the treatises "A Short History of the People Called Methodists"[40] and "Modern Christianity":

> I told them, "God has allowed me Liberty of Conscience, and so have the King and Parliament, and I hope my Neighbours will too; but if not, a Day is coming, when the Persecuted and the Persecutor shall stand together; and if you wrong me now, God will right me then."[41]

For John Wesley, the idea that new birth or regeneration would lead to a tranquil life is nowhere to be found. With Stovell, he considered "pain and struggle as part of the Christian journey." However, he did not teach to go looking for conflict. For example, in his diary he says: "We reached St. Ives about two in the morning. At five I preached on "Love your enemies"; and at Gewnnap, in the evening, on "All that will live godly in Christ Jesus

39 John Wesley, "Upon Our Lord's Sermon on the Mount" (no. 24), I.1.2.4; II.3; quoted from *Sermões de John Wesley: texto inglês com duas traduções em português*, ed. Helmut Renders et al (São Bernardo do Campo: Editeo, 2006), CD-ROM.

40 John Wesley, *A Short History of the People Called Methodists* (Halifax [s.e.], 1777), § 24, 34 e 101.

41 John Wesley, ed., *Modern Christianity: Exemplified at Wednesbury, and Other Adjacent Places in Staffordshire* (1745).

shall suffer persecution."[42] Overcoming the evil of human enmity by God's friendship is unfolded in the logic of reconciliation within society. Therefore, in "A Plain Account of Christian Perfection," he defines the ability to love humanity as Christian perfection, because it represents conformity to Christ.[43] According to Wesley, a holy people is an instrument in God's good hands, and so he prayed:

> Send forth thy blessed Spirit into the midst of these sinful nations, and make us a holy people: stir up the heart of our sovereign, of the royal family, of the clergy, the nobility . . . that they may be happy instruments in thy hand of promoting this good work. Be gracious to the universities, to the gentry and commons of this land . . . let the trial of their faith work patience in them. . . . Change the hearts of mine enemies, and give me grace to forgive them, even as thou for Christ's sake forgivest us."[44]

This last affirmation corresponds to the thought of Hannah Arendt. We now want to draw the metaphors of rebirth/regeneration close to her metaphor of "natality." Hannah Arendt uses this as a conceptual moment when a person is born into the political sphere, where acting with others can create something new and unexpected. According to Arendt, natality is tied to "three fundamental human activities: labor, work, and action," which correspond "to the biological process of the human body . . . to the unnaturalness of human existence . . . to the human condition of plurality."[45]

> Labor and work, as well as action, are also rooted in natality in so far as they have the task to provide and preserve the world for, to foresee and reckon with, the constant influx of newcomers. . . . However, of the three, action has the closest connection with the

---

42 Diary of John Wesley, June 22, 1745.

43 John Wesley, *A Plain Account of Christian Perfection as Believed and Taught by the Rev. Mr. John Wesley, from the Year 1725 to the Year 1765* (1766), §§ 10, 15 (5), e Q. 38.

44 John Wesley, *A Collection of Forms of Prayers for Every Day of the Week* (Bristol: [s.e.], 1742), 8.

45 Hannah Arendt, *The Human Condition*, 2nd ed. (Chicago: University of Chicago Press, 1998), 7.

> human condition of natality; the new beginning inherent in birth can make itself felt in the world only because the newcomer possesses the capacity of beginning something anew, that is, of acting. In this sense of initiative, an element of action, and therefore of natality, is inherent in all human activities.[46]

Arendt answers the question "being born for what?" with a vocation, a vocation to live together—plurality that requires action—actions of joint mutual care, which represents "political activity par excellence."[47] She says this relation is established by Genesis 1:27, that is, biblically, when it is affirmed that "male and female created he *them*."[48] In dialogue with Arendt, we want to ask: "being reborn for what?" We recall the question John Wesley has asked: "What may we reasonably believe to be God's design in raising up the Preachers called Methodists?" to which he answered: "to reform the nation, particularly the Church, and to spread holiness over the country." Arendt's emphasis on action as the key element in natality has affinity with Wesley's emphasis on action, including social, public, and political action, as an essential attribute of human beings seeking God and—after rebirth—aware that they belong to God.

Arendt criticizes the emphasis on quietness as part of "the enormous superiority of contemplation over activity of any kind, action not excluded," and classifies this emphasis as "not Christian in origin [but from] Plato's political philosophy." The understanding of freedom as "complete

---

46 Ibid., 9.

47 Ibid.

48 Ibid., 8. Arendt distinguishes between the first and second creation stories. "If we understand that this story of man's creation is distinguished in principle from the one according to which God originally created Man (*adam*), "him" and not "them," so that the multitude of human beings becomes the result of multiplication" (ibid.). We recall that the projection of "a new heaven and a new earth" in Revelation 21:3 also follows the logic of the first story of creation, when it affirms plurality of people will be preserved: "Look! God's dwelling place is now among the people, and he will dwell with them. They will be his people, and God himself will be with them and be their God." Arendt distinguishes, based on Jesus' preference for the first account and Paul's for the second, two types of faith: "For Jesus, faith was closely related to action . . . for Paul, faith was primarily related to salvation" (ibid., n. 1).

withdrawal from political activity" stems from a "philosophic *apolitia*" that preceded "the later Christian claim to be free from entanglement in worldly affairs,"[49] that is, political ones. Similarly, John Wesley rejects both Moravian attitudes of quietness by the Aldersgate religious society and a mysticism that focuses on the contemplative life (Aristotle's *bios theoretikos*) in favor of action and broad human initiative, which he generally describes as loving God, loving one's neighbor, and loving humanity. Admittedly, Hannah Arendt refers to a political standing in quite a different setting than Wesley, especially considering the possiblity of political involvement for the common people. However, the boundaries between public and private were not as fully defined then. Because of that, Wesley transcends the boundary of the religious, as found in Lutheran theology, referring in his writings not only to the members of the church or the people called Methodists but to humanity as a whole; he discusses the reforming of the country on different levels of "citizenship," sometimes within the bounderies of the established laws, sometimes questioning and pushing these bounderies to establish new laws, as shown by his relations to the parliament.[50]

Both Arendt and Wesley call into question inactivity and lack of initiative. In Wesley, new birth and regeneration do not limit themselves to an individualistic project but are a step toward the achievement of a broader project, including church and politics. Let us recall that his understanding of human beings as a reflection of the image of God states that the political image is considered a "rudimentary way in which humanity reflects its Maker. God endowed this creature with faculties for leadership and management,"[51] which involves, among other things, "liberty, a power of choice."[52] Wesley's metaphor for the image of God is close to Arendt's concept of natality. The metaphors of rebirth/regeneration refer to both the beginning of life and its

49 Ibid., 14–15.

50 Cf. Helmut Renders, *Andar Como Cristo Andou: Salvação Social em John Wesley*, 2nd ed., Revisada e ampliada (São Bernardo do Campo: Editeo, 2012), 54, 155, 167.

51 Theodore Runyon, *The New Creation: John Wesley's Theology Today*, (Nashville: Abingdon Press, 1998), 16.

52 Ibid., 17.

maturing. Thus, the metaphor of new birth/regeneration serves as a catalyst of that which Arendt describes as natality.

To summarize: Stovell's proposal represents an important reading for the life of the church. The experience of rebirth and the way of the cross are neither at odds nor endanger each other. In an increasingly bureaucratic and technological world—especially in our contemporary capitalist economies, in which emotions and desires are manipulated by a consumer industry—the experience of rebirth risks being transformed and reduced to a feeling of mere pleasure at God's proximity and intimacy, in a fatalistic understanding that God governs and maintains the world and human beings; we must guess at and contemplate his actions—preferably not interfering. This quietism or quietness—as not only the construction of personal salvation but also a collaboration of a new human being with the new creation—may be challenged by the appreciation of human natality in Arendt's sense. Human beings are divinely created and understood as beings who live in community, and, due to this plurality, are born tasked with being political entities whose activity must focus on the preservation and promotion of life.

However, this active and political being is not only a *homo faber.* According to Arendt, being political challenges the two grounds of totalitarianism: isolation and uprootedness.[53] Isolation is "that impasse into which men are driven when the political sphere of their lives, where they act together in the pursuit of a common concern, is destroyed."[54] Uprootedness means "to be uprooted . . . to have no place in the world, recognized and guaranteed by others; to be superfluous means not to belong to the world at all."[55] The struggle between isolation and uprootedness is clearly visible in Wesley's claim of the vocation of the Methodism movement: "to reform the nation, particularly the Church." The church is called to offer, internally, a place for roots that challenge uprootedness; and externally, the place for public commitment and the construction of alliances between social groups or classes

53 This idea is found in Celso Lafer, "A política e a condição humana," in Hannah Arendt, *The Human Condition*, 349.

54 Hannah Arendt, *The Origins of Totalitarianism* (New York: Harcourt, Brace, Jovanovich, 1973), 474.

55 Ibid.

and the institutions that represent them and that challenge isolation. Even more, the church can offer hope of reforming the nation—of constructing a public space worth living in and a source of pride. In Christian perspective, the gospel introduces important tools and perspectives of interaction to rebuild society: the way of reconciliation—as a proposal to overcome enmity by friendship; the way of pardon—as a way to empower victims; and the way of justice combined with mercy and humility—as a way to humanize society. By this, the church is in a position to continually reform itself or continue to "pour new wine into new wineskins" (Matt. 9:17 NIV).

Conclusion

The subject of new birth/regeneration is essential for the church to offer hope throughout life. Methodist and Wesleyan theologies, following John Wesley, call it the "way of salvation." From medieval to modern times, the notions of new birth/regeneration have focused on distinct aspects, especially baptism. This essay showed that there was a slow but increasing tendency to shift from being theocentric (and ecclesiocentric) in orientation (medieval theology) to a more anthropocentric-oriented theology (modern theology). If I am not mistaken, in contemporary, late-modernity we see the exhaustion of anthropocentrism in theology, expressed by practices that are more contemplative and tend to quietness.

The strong general emphasis on religious experience as transcendent offers a counterpoint to the alienating experience of the world of consumption (deception of desire *versus* satisfaction of desire) and media (simulation *versus* authenticity), forms that articulate this exhaustion of anthropocentrism, and, unfortunately, substitute for it a new radical theocentrism. This popularization of ecstatic experiences, at least in its middle-class and upper-class expressions, seems to follow and favor the old ideals of *bios theoretikos*. Whereas modernity dreamed about the rebirth of the Greco-Roman world, nowadays the dream of the rebirth of medieval times arises—or at least the annihilation of modernity and its respective pastoral practices and theology. In Brazil this dynamic has precedents in the pastoral practices and theologies of the Catholic Reformation, until its rebirth in the Ultramontane movement. In this tradition ecstatic religious experience is what experience is all about. Often, it is tied to the reception or contemplation of the Eucharist.

In this context the theology of John Wesley is helpful. It is an interesting legacy because it represents an attempt by a theology of mediation to answer the turn from medieval to modern times; the transition from a political world of absolute monarchy to constitutional monarchy; the transition from valuing aristocracy to valuing bourgeoisie; the transition of a mercantile system to a capitalist system. This is the world in which Wesley experiences God. For him, it was partially the medieval God—Anselm of Canterbury's wrathful God—but also the God who requires human collaboration in the construction of a new world. In our opinion this is part of Wesleyan theology's legacy: a theology that explores human existence in a shifting world, as an open process in and by which we interact with contemporary institutions and challenges and reread human experience and religious comprehension accumulated in history. This is a theology that holds on to the past but also moves in new directions by understanding present needs and intuiting ways to address them.

From scripture and tradition, and by experience, we learn that the gift of grace in and through which we have our being—physical and spiritual—is given freely, unconditionally, and universally. We believe that only this experience of grace is the basis for rebirth that propels us toward true humanization. We must explore a deeper relationship with God with a grateful heart as we commit to facing and assuming responsibility for our response to whatever happens. We must unite freedom and liberation *from* with freedom and liberation *for*, because unconditional, universal, and liberating grace, new birth, and regeneration are all invitations to live in the freedom offered by justification by faith. This means living the *shalom* of Christ instead of the *pax romana* of the world as constituents of our natality, strengthened by our rebirth and regeneration in Christ. The experience of regeneration promotes the development of a human being's character, whose knowledge, attitude, and vision can then collaborate in a world that will come to reflect the grace, peace, and beauty of God.

8

Let Us Hold Firmly to the Faith We Profess

Paulo Ayres Mattos

> Therefore, since we have a great high priest who has ascended into heaven, Jesus the Son of God, let us hold firmly to the faith we profess. For we do not have a high priest who is unable to empathize with our weaknesses, but we have one who has been tempted in every way, just as we are—yet he did not sin. Let us then approach God's throne of grace with confidence, so that we may receive mercy and find grace to help us in our time of need.
> —Hebrews 4:14-16 NIV

Hebrews: a letter that is no letter; it is a sermon. A sermon that does not end as a sermon; it ends as a letter. A letter-sermon that does not bear the name of its author or its recipients—whether an individual or a community. A letter-sermon whose internal evidences allow us no safe affirmation about where and when it was written. A letter-sermon written in sophisticated *koine* Greek, employing sophisticated Greek rhetoric that is very close to the Alexandrian Jewish school. A letter-sermon that, just as with the book of Revelation, employs a cyphered language, understandable by its recipients when written, but whose interpretative key became enigmatic for future generations. A letter-sermon that, contrary to classical interpretations that say it is a warning against the perils of Judaizing Christianity seduction, is actually a sermon-letter calling for resistance against both seduction and accommodation to Roman imperial domination that faced fourth- or fifth-generation Christian communities, comprised by men and women that had accepted Jesus of Nazareth as the Son of God.

Recent research on this letter-sermon known to us as the *Epistle to the Hebrews* concluded that its addressees lived the grace of the gospel under tremendous pressure by the Roman Empire. On the one hand, it expresses the possibility of cruel persecution, which early Christian generations suffered because of their profession of Jesus of Nazareth as *Kyrios*—Lord. On the other hand, it expresses the enormous attraction exerted by Roman societal values of honor, success, prestige, and social and economic prosperity.

Thus, what underlies the cyphered sacrificial language is not so much the peril of desertion and the necessity of going back to Jewish rites as it is the peril brought about by surrendering to Rome's imperial values. The letter-sermon addresses the pressures the Empire imposed upon men and women living within its boundaries by giving scathing criticism to those who were tempted to surrender to such pressures. To oppose the Empire, Hebrews employs images that were prevalent not only in late Judaism but particularly in Roman worship, which deified the emperor—well known to the recipients.

Thus, just as with Revelation, this letter-sermon was, above all else, a call to Christian men and women to resist the empire through their public witness to Jesus of Nazareth as Son of God. A call for them to oppose the authoritative "unique-discourse" imposed by the Roman Empire, with its claim of unquestionable power; an everlasting call that exerts the power of life and death under the guidance of the one true, victorious, and only *kyrios*-Lord—the person greeted by exclaiming: "Hail, Caesar!" This cyphered call was intelligible only by the recipients of this letter; a call that evokes the possibility of martyrdom for anyone who wishes to follow Jesus of Nazareth as Son of God—*Kyrios*. According to this letter-sermon, the price of the resistance against the emperor-*kyrios* would necessarily be martyrdom.

Thus, this letter-sermon is full of warnings against the temptation of abandoning faith in *Kyrios*-Jesus, who sits above the *kyrios*-emperor. This is why *Kyrios*-Jesus is a priest, not in accordance with the house of Aaron, but with the house of Melchizedek, which has no genealogy.

We place our reading of this letter-sermon in this context. Hebrews 4:14 presents us with a pleonasm of words when it affirms that Jesus of Nazareth is the Son of God, our great High Priest. This Jesus of Nazareth, Son of God, through his faithful witness, has ascended into heaven and entered the Most Holy Place and opened a new and living way to God, with no need for mediators between the Father and men and women. Barriers, walls, prejudices, marginalizing, and exclusions no longer have place. The affirmation of Jesus as the Son of God underlines the humanity of the Son of God—his humanization—in stark contrast to the divinization of the *kyrios*-emperor.

This letter-sermon uses the name "Jesus" just as much as the Greek title *Christos*, "Messiah." The Son of God, witnessed by Christian men and women, is Jesus of Nazareth, son of Mary, a carpenter's son. Previous passages mention divine filiation. Despite this, this passage deliberately introduces the title "Son of God" to its readers, relating his humanity in his divinity to his divinity in his humanity in a dynamic way.

In face of this Jesus-*Kyrios*, our great High Priest, the author of this letter-sermon exhorts us to "hold firmly to the faith we profess," to the confession of the church and its public witness. Here the need to witness publicly our confession of Jesus of Nazareth as *Christos-Kyrios* comes clearly to the forefront. In this case, confessing is much more than just publicly confessing our faith about baptism or declaring our faith in the historical symbols of the church. Rather, it is confessing our surrender to the lordship of Jesus of Nazareth as Son of God. We are called to publicly state the reason of our faith, a faith that has not been privatized by the lords of the empires of old or of today, but a faith that is lived and proclaimed in the streets and plazas of our lives.

The recipients of this letter-sermon received their faith from men and women of previous generations. These forebearers walked through the fires of persecution. Crazed men such as Nero dragged them into the cruel and public spectacles of the Roman Coliseum. Therefore, they knew the price they had to pay for their public witness to Jesus' name. Even now, our faith is tested and tried through our public confession of Jesus of Nazareth as Son of God. We prove ourselves, not by our Sunday rituals, or by our pious talk, or through performing signs and wonders. Rather, family, the streets, plazas, factories, schools, business and bank offices, palaces of governors, hospitals, radios, television, the Internet—the entire arena in which our lives play out—these are the places that test our faithfulness to Jesus-*Kyrios*. Here is where we face the possibility of betraying Jesus and deserting the values of the gospel.

It seems that the recipients of this letter-sermon were in danger of betraying and deserting their faith in Jesus the Son of God. So the writer of Hebrews tells us that we need to "hold firmly to the faith we profess." This demands we decide clearly whom we will serve and to which power we will subject ourselves. We also need strong political willpower, which is a clear indication of wanting and being able to publicly, openly, and unfalteringly affirm: "We must obey God rather than human beings" (Acts 5:29 NIV). We must face with unwavering and unflinching resolution any human empires, wherever, however, and whenever they rise up.

What, then, is the source of such resilience? The author of this letter-sermon answers us: "For we do not have a high priest who is unable to sympathize with our weaknesses, but we have one who in every respect has been tested as we are, yet without sin" (Heb. 4:15 NIV). This Jesus of Nazareth, confessed through the power of the Holy Spirit as the Son of God, our great High Priest, is flesh, bone, and blood—just like us.

Here the text comes full circle beginning in Hebrews 2:17:

> Therefore he had to become like his brothers and sisters in every respect, so that he might be a merciful and faithful high priest in the service of God, to make a sacrifice of atonement for the sins of the people.

Jesus of Nazareth, Son of God, is in solidarity with his people. The great High Priest "as we are," was tested "in every respect"—no more, no less. Because this Jesus of Nazareth, to whom we bear witness as the Son of God, is not separated from his humanity, even in his divinity. To the contrary, he is able to "sympathize" with our weaknesses in the face of imperial pressure, because he was tempted in every way, just as we are.

Instead of divinity separating him from our weaknesses and trials, drifting away from human needs, Jesus-*Kyrios* is always willing and able to suffer with us—to sympathize with our suffering—if we remain faithful to our confession and public witness of his lordship over our lives. Thus, he was, and is, able to be merciful toward us, because he knows from experience all possibilities. He can sympathize with the treason of Judas and the desertion by Peter.

The double negative in verse 15, "For we *do not* have a high priest who is *unable* to sympathize with our weaknesses," makes it clear that his solidarity with us is unrestricted and incessant. As one commentator on this letter-sermon says: Jesus-*Kyrios*, witnessed by the Spirit and by us as the Son of God,

> brings with him from that exalted sphere genuine compassion for the situation of his people, derived from his own earthly experience. The compassion [solidarity] of Christ, the exalted high priest, is not simply compassion that does not take human suffering into account, but a sentiment of one who faced and fully took it up.[1]

We evidently have here a Christology that goes from the least to the greatest, from the bottom up, from the base to the top. The fact that Christ did not sin was not the result of his divinity but of his resolve in facing and overcoming the temptations of both treason and desertion. For that, he relied on the promise that "man shall not live on bread alone, but on every word that comes from the mouth of God" (Matt. 4:4 NIV) and the assurance that we should worship only God (Matt. 4:10).

The fact that Jesus was tempted in every way, just like us, puts him in the same situation as ourselves when it comes to being faithful to the gospel. He experienced the same tensions and pressures that other human beings know. He is highly experienced in the trials of human life. The fact that Jesus of Nazareth overcame all trials is the guarantee that he is able to sympathize with us in all our weaknesses and help us overcome the temptation of both treason and desertion, our inclination to deny the gospel.

---

1 José Adriano Filho, *Peregrinos neste mundo: simbologia religiosa na Epístola aos Hebreus* (São Bernardo do Campo; São Paulo: Universidade Metodista de São Paulo; Loyola, 2001), 125–26.

The truth is that this letter-sermon points to the reality of the humanity of Jesus and the extent of his human experience. The fact is that Jesus opens to everyone a new and living way that "bases itself particularly in the presentation of the earthly experience of Jesus, and in his capacity to 'empathize with our weaknesses.'"[2] Moreover, the weaknesses that the author of Hebrews describes as resulting from faithful witness to the gospel are not mere moralistic or sentimental abstractions. Not at all! They are terribly concrete human experiences from daily life.

This is why we can boldly, confidently approach God's throne of grace from whence all divine mercy emanates toward all those who live this grace under pressure. This is where God gratuitously takes the initiative in our favor. It is freedom with neither fear nor dread, even though we know we cannot neglect so great a salvation. On the one hand, we have in this great High Priest a new and living way to God—Jesus of Nazareth, named "Son" by God himself. On the other hand, we have evidence that this God is merciful and ready to empower us in the face of all circumstances, despite the threats of this world's empires. Our access to God's merciful grace is unrestricted and without exclusion.

Therefore, Jesus' mercy comes out of his knowing all our weaknesses, because he can sympathize with all our needs, whatever they are. In fact, the grace of Jesus manifests more fully when we are under pressure from life's obstacles—whatever they are—when empires and the powerful try our faith and challenge our witness. Our great High Priest, Jesus of Nazareth, Son of God, knows our needs too well, and his grace is ever present, strengthening and empowering us to overcome the temptation to abandon our Lord and leave our community of faith. The assurance of his amazing grace comes to our rescue when pressure bears down on us.

Just as was true for the recipients of the Epistle to the Hebrews, empires still pressure us as communities of faith that follow Jesus of Nazareth, calling us to live in God's grace even under pressure. It is then that we may more fully experience Jesus' solidarity with us.

The Epistle to the Hebrews still is a call to oppose the "unique-discourse" imposed upon us by empires and their claims to unquestionable power: to

2 Ibid., 126.

last forever, exerting power of life and death over all under their control. Our guide is the one true, victorious, and only *Kyrios*-Lord. This letter-sermon's call may have been intelligible only to those who received it, but as part of the church, we do understand. It was a call that evoked the possibility of martyrdom for those who were willing to follow Jesus of Nazareth the Son of God—*Kyrios*. This we also understand. "Whoever has ears, let them hear what the Spirit says to the churches." (See Rev. 2:7, 11, 17, 29 NIV.)

As a community of faith that follows Jesus of Nazareth, we face the treason and desertion of many people who are tempted to surrender to the seductions of the empire and its fallacious promises of prestige, success, and wealth to all its followers. The price of this submission is corruption in all areas of social life, from politics to religion. Despite the fact that churches are also tempted to become colonies of the empire, Hebrew's exhortation rings with all the more urgency and relevance: "Let us then approach God's throne of grace with confidence, so that we may receive mercy and find grace to help us in our time of need" (Heb. 4:16 NIV).

May God help us! Amen.

Index

www.ingramcontent.com/pod-product-compliance
Lightning Source LLC
LaVergne TN
LVHW030921080826
845145LV00013B/3005

* 9 7 8 1 7 9 1 0 4 3 3 4 6 *